U.S. Dept. of the Treasury, James W. Taylor

Report of James W. Taylor

on the mineral resources of the United States east of the Rocky mountains

- 1867

U.S. Dept. of the Treasury, James W. Taylor

Report of James W. Taylor
on the mineral resources of the United States east of the Rocky mountains - 1867

ISBN/EAN: 9783337187125

Printed in Europe, USA, Canada, Australia, Japan

Cover: Foto ©Suzi / pixelio.de

More available books at **www.hansebooks.com**

REPORT

OF

JAMES W. TAYLOR,

ON THE

MINERAL RESOURCES

OF THE

UNITED STATES EAST OF THE ROCKY MOUNTAINS.

WASHINGTON:
GOVERNMENT PRINTING OFFICE.
1868.

LETTER

THE SECRETARY OF THE TREASURY,

TRANSMITTING

Report on the mineral resources of the United States east of the Rocky mountains.

MAY 2, 1868.—Referred to the Committee on Mines and Mining, and ordered to be printed.

TREASURY DEPARTMENT,
Washington, May 2, 1868.

SIR : I transmit herewith to the House of Representatives the report of James W. Taylor on the mineral resources of the States and Territories east of the Rocky mountains.

Very respectfully, your obedient servant,

HUGH McCULLOCH,
Secretary of the Treasury.

Hon. SCHUYLER COLFAX,
Speaker of the House of Representatives.

REPORT

OF

JAMES W. TAYLOR,

ON

THE MINERAL RESOURCES OF THE UNITED STATES EAST OF THE ROCKY MOUNTAINS.

WASHINGTON, *May* 2, 1868.

SIR: In pursuance of your instructions of September 12, 1866, I had the honor on the 13th of February, 1867, to present for your consideration a preliminary report, embracing a general view of the gold and silver districts of New Mexico, Colorado, Montana, Dakota, and Minnesota, with some notice of the gold regions of the southern Atlantic states, Canada and Nova Scotia. The present report will include a further inquiry into the mineral resources of those districts, with special reference to their situation and prospects at the expiration of the year 1867; and I propose as a not inappropriate sequel to devote a considerable portion of this communication (1) to a general review of the production of gold and silver in other quarters of the world, with the purpose of indicating relatively the commercial and social importance of the treasure product of the United States, and (2) to a summary of the domestic commerce from the Mississippi river westward to the interior or mining districts of the United States, having reference prominently to railway communications with the Rocky mountains and the Pacific coast.

THE GREAT PLAINS.

Between the agricultural districts of Dakota, Nebraska, Kansas, Indian territory, and Texas, which extend westwardly to the 98th meridian of longitude, and the eastern Piedmont of the Rocky mountains, and in Colorado are bounded eastwardly by longitude 104°, the cretaceous formation, once designated as the "American desert," is now well understood to be adequate for the sustenance of cattle, and if subterranean sources of water supply were available for the purpose of irrigation, might become an agricultural region. At present this wide interval between the margin of the Missouri river, where the moist winds from the Gulf of Mexico afford a sufficient fall of summer rain for the growth and maturity of crops, and the Colorado Piedmont, with its limited capacity for irrigation from mountain streams and surfaces, is recognized as a grazing district, bearing the nutritious buffalo grass, and reasonably traversed by streams—conditions only favorable to pastoral occupation and a sparse population. If, however, the experiment of artesian wells should be vigorously prosecuted, and prove successful, the occupation of the plains might be greatly diversified. The government in 1858 despatched a party under the direction of Captain John Pope to the Llano Estacado of western Texas, an extension of the cretaceous formation of eastern Colorado, for the purpose of sinking an artesian well; but although a depth of 1,050 feet was attained, and powerful streams flowed into the well at different levels, the water did not rise to the surface, and the work was abandoned. It was by no means a failure; the discovery of subterranean streams or fountains accessible, from the surface, being very suggestive of the possibilities of future water supply.*

NEW MEXICO.

During 1867 the public attention was occupied by very favorable reports of the mineral resources of New Mexico. The Kansas division of the Union Pacific railroad, while not relinquishing the policy of a direct western communication with Denver and Great Salt Lake City, determined to place a party in the field to explore a southwestern line from the junction of longitude 102° with latitude 39° to a crossing of the Rio Grande at Albuquerque, latitude 35°, longitude 106½°, and thence westwardly through New Mexico, Arizona, and southern California, on or near the 35th parallel.

The results of this exploration fully confirming the observations of Lieutenant Whipple in 1853–'54, have established that gold, silver, and copper mines are as numerous and valuable as in Colorado; and also that beds of lignite·coal occur around the western end of Raton mountain, and the neighboring foot-hills of the Rocky mountains, while a formation of early cretaceous coal has been discovered in the valley of the Rio Grande. The first coal basin consists of an immense thickness of coarse sandstones, first manifesting themselves in some of the ravines of the Raton, about 20 miles east of Raton Pass, but soon becoming visible on the flanks of the mountain, continuing through the pass, and to an unknown distance west of it. This formation lies nearly horizontally against the base of the Raton and Rocky mountains, extending the latter from the Arkansas river at Cañon City to the valley of the Little Cimarron on the south. In the Raton Pass the coal beds, which are quite thin in the Manco del Barro Pass, begin to assume importance. About six miles from Trinidad, a locality exhibits a total thickness of about five feet of good coal, separated into four beds, placed near together. Near the top of the pass are also beds of the same thickness, but at the southern exit of the pass, in cañons connected with upper waters of the Canadian, there called Red river, these beds occur in still greater magnitude, being eight feet thick. All these are, however, of trifling nature compared with the great beds found in the cañons of the Vermejo valley, which show in one locality 10 feet of coal in two beds, separated by 10 inches of slate. The same strata were found on the other side of the cañon, one-half mile distant, and in other cañons several miles westward. Further south other thinner beds were seen near Vermejo of the thickness of three and four feet of good coal. Beyond the Pernejo the high table lands containing the coal beds disappear entirely, and the only sedimentary rock in view is the early cretaceous·sandstone, capped in places with middle cretaceous limestone. As the high table land of tertiary sandstone extends north of the Raton, it is probable that similar beds exist in that direction. Coal has also been discovered on the Rio Grande in various places above Piedras Negras, as well as below in the vicinity of Laredo, Gurrero, and Roma.†

The discoveries of gold-bearing quartz, first limited to the Gregory district, in Colorado, extending about 30 miles along the base of the Snowy range, from Gold Hill to Empire City, now reach the southern limit of Colorado, and thence along the Sierra Madre, following the general course of the valley of the Rio

---

* In 1867, at Chicago an artesian well, at the depth of 1,190 feet, struck a subterranean stream, eight feet in depth, and flowing with a strong current, from which 600,000 gallons daily are delivered at the surface, and 450,000 gallons daily at an elevation of 45 feet. Previously a vein of water had been reached at a depth of 90 feet, which yielded 15 barrels an hour. (See Appendix No. 1 for a narrative by Professor D. D. Owen of other experiments within the United States and elsewhere.)

† The value of coal in the reduction of ores, as well as for uses of fuel, justifies all possible details of the recent discoveries in the Rocky mountains. The foregoing report is by Dr. J. L. Le Conte, who accompanied General W. W. Wright, chief engineer of Union Pacific railway, eastern division, upon the expedition already mentioned.

Grande through the whole extent of New Mexico and into the adjacent State of Chihuahua. Successful placer mining by the Mexican residents of this valley has often been reported in the mountain gulches near Santa Fé, south to a distance of about 100 miles, or as far as Gran Quivira, and north for about 120 miles to the river Sangre de Cristo. This stream is just within the territory of Colorado, but 20 miles south of the boundary line is the locality of the Moreno mines, which attracted much attention during 1867. They are situated near but west of the Raton mountains, about 30 miles north of Taos, Moro county, New Mexico. Four pounds of the ore from a well-defined quartz vein recently opened are said to have yielded 78 cents of gold, or at the rate of $390 to the ton. An important circumstance is added, that the quartz contains only free gold, without sulphurets. In a specimen taken from the vicinity of the surface and forwarded to Colorado, thread gold could be traced through the mass of quartz. The opportunities for gulch mining have already attracted a considerable American population. The Placer mountain, about 30 miles from Santa Fé, within the past year has been worked under an efficient organization and with satisfactory results. The average yield of the auriferous rock is $30 to the ton. The veins are numerous, well defined, and accessible within a district of 10 miles square. Another locality of much interest is Pinos Altos, under latitude 33°, longitude 108°. The enterprise of working these mines seems to be under efficient direction. Upon one of the lodes a tunnel has already been drifted 713 feet, and when completed to the distance of 1,600 feet, will have passed from the Atlantic to the Pacific slopes of the Sierra Madre. Midway it passes under the crest of the mountain, from which a shaft of 121 feet connects the summit with the tunnel. The ore contains gold, silver, and a small proportion of copper. The village of Pinos Altos is at an elevation of 5,000 feet above the sea. The vicinity presents unusual advantages of wood, water, and surface for mining operations, and, with the fullest allowance for exaggeration as to the number and richness of the lodes, there seems but little doubt that, with the pacification of the Indian tribes and further facilities of transportation, it will become an important mining centre.

The foregoing seem to be the most prominent gold-bearing districts of New Mexico; but some 20 localities are mentioned by mining journals, among which are quartz veins at San José, in the Sierra Madre, intersecting each other in all directions for a mile in width and three miles in length; a similar formation near Fort Davis, Texas, and extensive placer mines on the San Francisco and Mimbres rivers.

Silver, however, with its many combinations, is the most abundant mineral of the Territory. The prominently argentiferous districts are the Placer mountains, near Santa Fé; the Organ mountains, near the Mesilla valley; and the Sierra Madre, at Pinos Altos. The first and last of these localities are, as we have seen, gold-producing also. In the Organ mountains over 50 silver mines have been discovered, the ore being generally argentiferous galena. The district near Mesilla valley, in the Organ mountains, has a mean altitude of 4,400 feet, and is intersected with ravines, affording favorable opportunities for horizontal drifts in opening the veins. The country bordering on the north portion of Chihuahua is a rich silver district. Immediately adjoining the Mexican boundary are the mines of Corralitos, the most successful silver mines in the State of Chihuahua, having been mined for 40 years in a region most exposed to Indian hostility. Near the old town of El Paso tradition places the locality of one of the richest silver mines known to the Spaniards, but its site was lost during the Indian insurrection of 1680.

Dr. A. Wizlizenns, who accompanied a military expedition in 1847 as surgeon and naturalist, mentions that during the Spanish occupation several rich silver mines were worked at Avo, at Cerillos, and in the Nambe mountains, but none at present. Copper is found in abundance throughout the country, but principally at Los Tijeras, Jemas, Abiquin, Guadelupita de Mora. Iron is equally abundant. Gypsum, both common and selenite, is found in large quantities, extensive layers of it existing in the mountains near Algodones, on the Rio Grande, and in the neighborhood of the celebrated Salinas. It is used as common lime, and the crystalline or selenite is a substitute for window glass. About 100 miles southeast of Santa Fé, on the high table land between the Rio Grande and Pecos, are some extensive salt lakes or salinas, from which the inhabitants of New Mexico are supplied.

The leading copper mines of New Mexico may be thus enumerated and described: 1. Hanover, discovered in 1860; situated on the headwaters of the Mimbres river, about six miles east of Fort Bayard; ore a virgin copper, found in extensive pockets in the bed rock, varying in quantities from 100 to 300 pounds, and combined with sufficient gold to defray the expenses of working. 2. Santa Rita, in the same vicinity, worked by the Spaniards nearly a century and a half ago; ore a rich oxide, and found in veins of varying thickness, the lower being virgin copper, which can be drawn under the hammer as it comes from the mine; supposed to be an extension of the Hanover. 3. Pinos Altos, associated with the extensive gold and silver formation previously mentioned; a very extensive copper deposit, and favorably situated in respect to wood and water. 4. Arroyo Honda, situated north of Taos and close to the Colorado line, from which specimens of copper have been exhibited at the United States mint and pronounced equal to the amygdaloid of Lake Superior. 5. Naciemento, situated about 40 miles south-southwest from Santa Fé, in the Los Valles mountains, in the same range as the Placer mountain; vein from 30 to 40 feet wide, and occasionally intersected by deposits of white sandstone; assay of ore, copper, 71; silver, 4; iron, 12; unexamined scoria, 13. 6. Ocate, near Santa Fé, vein 12 to 20 feet wide and assays 64 per cent. of pure copper. 7. Tijera, situated in the Tijera cañon, near the line of the 35th parallel; surface ore alloyed with silver, but in descending the copper combines with gold. 8. New Mexico, a formation of the Placer mountain, very extensive, and under the same administration as the gold mines of that locality. For many years much of the copper ore of New Mexico has been transported to Indianola, Texas, a distance of 1,000 miles, and the amount of the gold associated with the copper has always been sufficient to defray the expenses of transportation.*

COLORADO.

This interesting Territory has been fortunate during the ,year just closed in the publication of an attractive picture of its mountain scenery, by Bayard Taylor; an exhaustive work upon its "mining organizations and prospects," by O. J. Hollister; and a careful collation of its mineral and other products at the Paris Exposition, under the direction of Commissioner J. P. Whitney. Very free reference will be made to these authentic sources of information.

The agricultural section of Colorado, called by its people the valley, extends eastward from the base of the Rocky mountains, with an area of 30,000,000 acres, of which one-sixth is susceptible of irrigation, and is therefore arable. The next division is the Foot-hills with its subdivision, the great mineral belt. Then follows the Snowy range, or the range with its system of parks—the crest or sierra of the mountain mass—while "over the range" includes all west of the continental divide. The entire area is 103,475 square miles, or 67,723,520 acres.

Until recently the gold formation of the Foot-hills was the first object of interest to mineralogists after leaving the plains; but, with the extension of the Union Pacific railway, the probability of an adequate coal formation fully divides attention. With the exploration of the valleys which debouch from the

---

* Letter to Philadelphia Press from member of Pacific Railway exploration in 1867.

first elevations of the Rocky mountains a lignite has been discovered upon the Yellowstone of Montana, the Platte of Colorado, and the Rio Grande of New Mexico, while within the parks at a greater elevation deposits are found similar to the Albertine coal of New Brunswick upon the Atlantic coast. It is not unlikely that the bituminous beds of Iowa and Missouri, disappearing under the cretaceous masses of the plains, may reappear with the upheaval of the mountains in a condition highly metamorphosed, if not in the form of anthracite. The veins of lignite first mentioned have a general direction north and south along the base of the mountains, and are accessible where the mountain streams traverse the Foot-hills.

The most prominent discovery of coal in Colorado is on South Boulder creek, about two miles from the base of the mountains, 15 miles from Denver, and 15 miles from Golden City, the latter being the centre of the gold mining district. In regard to the character and quality of this deposit Dr. J. V. Hayden, United States geologist, reports that there are at least 10 beds from 5 to 13 feet in thickness, belonging to the tertiary period and of the lignite variety. It is non-bituminous and holds a position between dry wood and the anthracites of Pennsylvania ; burns with a bright red flame, giving abundant heat and very little ash—2 per cent. of ash and 58 of carbon. Associated with these coal beds are veins of iron ore of the red or brown hematite. The value of coal and iron deposits, with reference to the construction and use of machinery for reducing and smelting ores, is quite apparent.*

The localities in which gold is most plentifully found are in the counties of Boulder, Gilpin, Clear Creek, Jefferson, and the extreme southeastern part of Summit. Although it is evident that many other sections contain gold-bearing veins no great amount of attention has been bestowed upon them, and the principal amount of mining has been done in the counties of Gilpin and Clear Creek. The gold veins proper, found wholly in granite formation, vary in width from a scarcely perceptible streak to 40 and even 50 feet, but seldom averaging over four or five feet. When discovered from the surface the vein is indicated by a light porous quartz, discolored by the oxidation of base metals, in which small particles of gold are disseminated sometimes in the form of small scales, fine dust, or stringy pieces, but seldom in masses of any size. The value of veins is usually determined by the miners by crushing to a fine powder in a hand mortar a few pieces of surface ore, the powder being carefully washed with water in a hand pan. This consists in giving the pan a peculiar motion which settles the gold at the bottom, the fine particles of earth and quartz being carefully floated off. It is seldom that surface ore is found so poor as not to exhibit from a few pieces so treated, a streak of fine gold dust at the bottom of the pan. From some veins pieces can be readily found, by a little search, showing specks of gold up to the size of pin heads. Sometimes streaks of white and yellow earths are found in surface ores, which yield from $5 to $60 to the panful of 12 or 15 pounds. When such streaks are found large amounts are often obtained from them. The surface ore, generally quite soft and porous at the top, gradually grows harder and more compact as it recedes from the oxidizing effects of the atmosphere, and is finally lost in the glittering sulphurets of iron and copper which takes its place, being equally rich in gold, and oftentimes a vast deal richer, having in addition a large percentage of silver, and oftentimes an amount of copper equivalent to 25 per cent. of bulk. The surface ore, when found in veins of ordinary width and richness, is stripped from the veins, until the sulphurets are met with, and is submitted to the ordinary process of amalgamation on large copper plates coated with quicksilver, or in large iron or wooden pans, the ore being scoured by revolving spars of iron or masses of stone.

---

* See appendix No. 2 for an abstract of Professor Hayden's observations on "The Lignites of the West," originally published in Silliman's Journal of March, 1869.

In this manner surface ores are made to pay good profits, and in some instances very large amounts.

The tracts containing gold veins, designated as belts, seem to have a uniform course northeast by southwest, cropping out in some localities, and then disappearing from the surface to be found beyond in their continuation. In places, by some natural convulsions of nature at an early period, they are broken and distorted from the regularity which marks them elsewhere, and for acres in extent the surface of the earth is discolored by the peculiar blossom which indicates the presence of sulphurets below. Such tracts, when water can be brought to them, are sluiced to great profit.

A peculiarity of the Colorado gold veins is that they are invariably found richer the deeper they are sunk upon. This rule seems to be without exception, and in no instance is a vein lost except by a break-off in the adjoining formation. Gold is not found to any great extent in a free state after leaving the surface ores. The great percentage of the precious metal is found intimately associated with the sulphurets of iron, copper, silver, lead, antimony, and arsenic. Iron predominates over the other metals, often comprising from 30 to 40 per cent. of the crevice matter. Copper is almost invariably represented, and few veins show less than from three to five per cent. of this metal, and many exhibit from 15 to 20 per cent. This metal increases almost invariably as the veins are sunk upon, showing a tendency to assume the form of sulphate as it descends. In the copper, particularly the sulphate, is found the greatest percentage of gold, often giving an assay exceeding $2,000 to the ton of 2,000 pounds. Miles of shafts have been sunk and tunnels run in Colorado, but no single shaft or tunnel has yet attained any great depth.

Shafts have been sunk upon the Gold Dirt, Bobtail, and Gregory lodes, to a depth of between 300 to 400 feet, in every instance exhibiting ore of surpassing richness. The great majority of shafts, however, from want of means and from ignorance of the true method of treating the ores found, have not been sunk more than sufficiently deep to demonstrate the value of the lodes they are upon.

The gold-mining regions are easily reached from the plains below, and are connected by good roads. Streams, having sufficient water and fall to furnish unlimited power for mining purposes, are plentiful. The valleys and agricultural lands, though being less sheltered and productive than those upon the western side of the range or the plains below, are sufficiently fertile to furnish more than a much larger population can consume. Timber, also, is plentiful, and the climate, though uncertain in its temperature during the summer, is not attended in winter with that severity which is peculiar to the Atlantic sea-coast towns of the same latitude.

Within the last year a considerable quantity of ore, taken from several mines, was freighted across the plains to the river, and forwarded to Swansea, in Wales, that it might be experimented upon by the skilled experience employed there. No difficulty was found in working the ore in Swansea, which gave yields of between $200 and $300 to the ton, the same ore not yielding over $10 or $15 to the ton by the stamp-and-pan mills in Colorado, yet paying a profit from that amount.

No accurate estimates can be made of the amount of gold obtained from Colorado, particularly during the earlier days, owing to the irregular methods of remitting in vogue ; but probably not less than $30,000,000 have been obtained within the limits of the Territory from 1859 up to the present time—not a large amount when compared with the yield from other more advanced mining regions during the same time, but a large sum considering the small number of people engaged in obtaining it, their isolation from settled regions, their Indian difficulties, and the destructive influences of the civil war raging at the same time in the United States.

Silver is found in all the gold mining districts of Colorado, associated with the ores containing gold, in the galena particularly, which is found at times in considerable quantity. It is always present, but not sufficiently plentiful to be a feature of value in the gold mines; yet large masses have lately been obtained by the smelting process from ores considered strictly gold-bearing, and it is quite evident that in future, with the advantages of improved processes, this metal will be freely obtained. But not until within the last two years was it generally known in Colorado that immense belts of silver veins, separate from the gold, existed upon the western declivities of the Rocky Mountain range, corresponding in their direction and general features with those of gold upon the eastern side. The prevailing great richness in silver in the ores of Griffith and Argentine districts, in Clear Creek county, upon the head waters of South Clear creek, some 13 miles distant from the towns of Central and Black Hawk, and correspondingly near to the snowy peaks of the range, first attracted particular attention to the element of silver. In these districts silver ores of great richness have been discovered, masses being exhibited at the Paris Exposition from the Baker lode, of Argentine district, and of the Elijah Hise and Indigo lodes, of Griffith district, which assay respectively, in silver alone, $532 12, $1,656 20, and $1,804 83 to the ton of 2,000 pounds of ore. These veins were followed to an altitude previously unknown in mining experience in Colorado. Enterprising men were soon engaged in prospecting the regions corresponding upon the other side of the range, which resulted in the discovery of immense deposits of rich argentiferous galena. The black sulphurets of silver, antimonial silver ores, rich chlorides, ruby silver ore, and pieces of native silver were found, and a new region, the extent of which has not yet been determined, was thrown open to the attention of those who might have the curiosity to examine it.

Much excitement was occasioned in Colorado by this discovery, and a large number of prospectors were soon engaged there, making discoveries and pre-emptions under the liberal laws of the Territory, which gave undisputed possession to discoverers who should have their claims recorded in the county office, after making the developments and improvements required by law.

That portion of the silver region first opened is situated in Summit county, upon the head waters of the Snake and Swan rivers, which flow into the Blue river, a tributary of the Rio Colorado, which flows into the Gulf of California. An examination of the region a few miles southwest, in the neighborhood of Ten Mile creek, another tributary of the Blue, led to the discovery of still more wonderful exhibits of mineral wealth than were found in the Snake river region. Veins of great width and prominence were found, which, in some instances, could be distinguished by their discolored surface ores, when miles distant, seaming the mountain sides like gigantic roads, measuring from 20 to 50 feet in width. In this region the result of violent volcanic action is evident by the great height of many peaks, their abrupt and broken sides, and by the immense masses of lava and scoria which abound. Not far distant are hot saline and sulphur springs, as well as deposits of dry salt.

Fletcher mountain, in Ten-mile district, where the richest mines yet discovered are found, may be designated, if the application be a proper one, the predominant peak or watershed of the continent. From each side of this mountain rise streams, (Gilpin and Clinton,) which, flowing into Ten Mile creek, empty into the Grand, and then into the Rio Colorado—in fact, being the head waters and origin of that great stream which, originating at an altitude of over two miles above tide-water, in a region teeming with mineral wealth, seeks the shores of the Pacific through a region which is one vast field of metallic treasure, but which lies deserted, neglected, and comparatively unknown. Upon the western, near the base, are numerous rivulets, emptying into the Blue, another tributary of the Rio Colorado. Southward from Fletcher mountain a few miles, so near Ten Mile creek that the waters almost mingle, rises the Arkansas river, flowing into the Mississippi. To the south, not many miles further, rise the head waters of the Rio Grande del Norte, flowing into the Gulf of Mexico. At the south-eastern base of Fletcher mountain rises the South Platte river, which, striking north, circles over the great plains, irrigating the soil in its passage, and supplying water to tens of thousands who yearly make their migrations to the promising lands of the far west.

During the short time which has elapsed since the discovery of the silver mining regions good roads have been made, connecting them with the more settled sections of the Territory, from Snake river mines to Denver, by way of Breckinridge, the county-seat of Summit county, and from Ten Mile district to Denver, by way of the Arkansas river and the South Park. In both sections a large number of shafts have been sunk upon the principal rivers to a depth of from 20 to 60 feet, some of which have exhibited an abundance of rich ore. In Ten Mile district miners were engaged during the past winter—in the employ of eastern capitalists, who subscribed a large sum for the purpose—in driving a tunnel from the base of Fletcher mountain to its centre, for the purpose of ascertaining, from ore taken at a great depth, the true value of veins which presented such indications of wealth upon the surface. This tunnel, commencing at a height of about 60 feet above the water-line of the district, had been driven through the solid rock (of which the mountains, beneath a thin coating of earth, are almost entirely composed) to a depth of about 300 feet, and will be steadily prosecuted until it reaches, at a depth of from 600 to 800 feet, a large vein known as the Campton, which exhibits upon the surface, for over a mile in length, a crevice, which has a uniform width of 10 feet, and which has given from shafts sunk upon it some of the richest ore obtained in the district.

From the silver mines of Summit county 76 assays were made during the past year by Albert Reichenecker, a graduate of the Polytechnic School of the kingdom of Wurtemburg, and who served the state government of that kingdom nine years as chemist and engineer of mines, who obtained an average assay of $121 64 to the ton of 2,000 pounds; and deposes that said ores taken for assay were only a fair average of the ore from the mines from which they were respectively taken, and that they came from a depth not exceeding 20 feet, and in most cases from within five feet of the surface.

From 30 assays, made by Fred. Eckfeldt, melter and refiner at the United States branch mint at Denver, an average assay was obtained of $130 28 to the ton of 2,000 pounds; Eckfeldt deposing that the ores so assayed were but a fair average of the mines from which they were taken.

The silver mining regions abound in many streams, which have their sources in the immense masses of snow found always upon the high mountain peaks. These streams, being fed by thousands of small rivulets and springs, gain in a short distance immense force and volume, giving unfailing freshness to the rich grasses, flowers, wild fruits, and lofty trees found in the valleys they traverse.

At a height of 12,000 feet, in these regions, timber disappears, though rich pasturage and flowers are found growing close to the banks of snow. Strawberries are often found growing in great abundance far above the timber line, as well as raspberries. The timber above an altitude of 8,000 or 9,000 feet is principally fir and spruce, which is quite abundant, and grows to a great size. The native grass is of an extremely nutritious quality, and for hay cannot be excelled. It grows high and vigorously, and in the valleys and parks can be cut in great quantities. Trout are found in the streams at a height of nearly 12,000 feet, and a variety of wild game is abundant. The climate is less severe in the silver regions than at the same altitudes upon the eastern side of the range, owing to the high mountains which intervene, and which form barriers against the sweeping winds of the plains. Settlements are rapidly being made in those sections, and soon they will resound with the busy labor of thousands who will be required to develop the wonderfully rich and accessible treasures of which now the existence is comparatively unknown.

Lead, in the form of galena, exhibits itself in many of the gold mines, but diminishes in quantity as the shafts sink. It is more plentifully found in Ten-mile district, Summit county, than in any other section yet known. In that district it is in some instances found projecting in large masses above the surface of the earth upon the line of vein, and can be detached in a partially oxidized condition in pieces weighing from 500 to 1,000 pounds. Upon Fletcher mountain thousands of tons could be easily gleaned from the surface, and but a short distance below the surface are large beds, the extent of which have not yet been determined. This galena is never found free from silver, yielding from 10 to 500 ounces to the ton of metal.

From some pieces of galena, fair average ors from a number of veins in Ten-mile district, the following assays for silver were obtained by Professor A. A. Hayes, State assayer of Massachusetts:

		Oz.	Dwts.	Grs.
Pyramid vein	per ton 2,000 pounds..	81	13	8
Merrimac vein	do	68	12	0
Polygon vein	do	266	8	0
Hard Cash vein	do	108	2	12
Blackstone vein	do	85	18	6
Young vein	do	65	6	16
Finsley vein	do	178	17	0
Siberian vein	do	106	9	20
Augustine vein	do	221	3	12

giving an average exceeding 130 ounces to the ton.

This metal, like copper, has not been mined for, excepting for the purpose of obtaining it to flux other metals with by the new smelting process.

Deposits of dry salt are found in some parts of the Territory, and salt springs are quite plentiful in the parks. The salt found in a dry state is comparatively pure, and the saline springs contain fully one-half pound of salt to the gallon of water. Some of the springs are very large. In the South Park extensive works are erected and in operation for boiling and evaporating the brine. The spring from which the works are supplied is some 1,000 feet long by 150 feet wide, from the bottom of which the water boils up vigorously.

The following are altitudes above the sea of some towns and passes in Colorado:

	Feet.
Denver City	5,317
Golden City	5,882
Central City	8,300
Idaho	7,800
Georgetown	8,452
Empire City	8,871
Pass over the range via Cheyenne	7,500
Pass over the range via Berthond	10,914
Pass over the range via South Park	11,000
Pass over the range via Boulder	11,700
Pass over the range via Jones	12,200
Pass over the range via Argentine	13,000
North, South, Middle, and San Luis Parks, from	6,000 to 9,000
Main belts of gold mines, from	7,000 to 9,000
Main belts of silver mines, from	8,000 to 11,000

About one-half of the Territory is covered with timber, the growth in some sections being small and scattering, composed of the piñon, or nut-bearing pine, and scrubby cedar. These are confined to the lower foot-hills of the mountains. Higher up are found cedar, spruce, fir, and pine, which grow to an enormous size. Hemlock, aspen, and oak are also found. Plum and cherry trees are met with growing wild, and the apple and pear are being cultivated with success. Wild grapes, strawberries, raspberries, and currants are abundant, and heavy growths of wild clover, wild rye, and wild barley cover many of the valleys.

The records of the United States Land Office exhibit sales of 210,000 acres of farming land in the Territory, with 190,000 acres claimed but not paid for, making 400,000 acres under improvement. Of this number 100,000 acres are well cultivated. Wheat, barley, and oats yield from 30 to 70 bushels to the acre, and all varieties of vegetables are successfully raised. In 1865, for a number of months corn and oats sold readily at prices ranging from 15 to 25 cents per pound. In the summer of 1866 grains sold in Colorado at prices less than those ruling in Chicago, Illinois, the largest grain mart in the world. Eight or ten flour mills are now in operation, which are making more flour than the people of the Territory can consume.

Enough has been done in Colorado to satisfy any one of the true value of the countless and inexhaustible veins which so closely pack and seam her mountain sides, and the improvements which have been made there in so short a time must appear astonishing to any one who will examine them. But the great difficulties which have been encountered must be taken into consideration by those who review her mining processes; the interruptions of the war and Indian difficulties; the long distance and high rates of freight from the Missouri river, and the delay occasioned in getting the machinery ordered, which, being of novel construction, had to be manufactured expressly for the purpose. But these difficulties are happily now overcome by the cessation of war, by the building of railroads, and by the manufacturing establishments in the Territory, so that we may reasonably expect in the succeeding few years to see a more rapid and successful advance.

WYOMING, OR LINCOLN.

On the organization of Montana Territory, and the limitation of Idaho to districts west of the Rocky mountains, a region remained south of Montana which, for want of settlements or any form of public organization, was annexed to Dakota. It will probably be constituted a Territory at the current session of Congress, as important discoveries of gold mines have lately occurred in the valley of the Sweetwater and on the sources of the Wind river. The Cereso lode, near the South Pass, is the most prominent locality, and was the first scene of discovery. As much as $130 per day is claimed as the reward of one man's labor with a hand mortar. Some 150 lodes have been located, all within a circle of 6 by 15 miles, while the great mineral belt in which the mines are found extends from Frémont's Peak south to the junction of Grand and Green rivers. There seems to be little doubt that the foot-hills of the Wind River mountains are equally auriferous.

The Sweetwater mines are situated northeast of the old emigrant road which leads through South Pass and by the Pacific Springs, and are on the eastern slope of the Rocky mountains; and thus far only one ledge has been observed to cross the divide to the western slope of the mountains. The line of the Pacific road is 25 miles south of the mines—the telegraph within nine miles. A population of 600 passed the winter of 1867–'68 in this district; a newspaper, the Sweetwater Miner, has commenced its issues, and the federal government will probably be represented by territorial officers at an early day.

MONTANA.

So much interest is expressed in the mining development of this new Territory that I have sought and obtained the valuable assistance of W. S. Keyes, mining engineer, a resident of Montana, to present with some detail the narratives of mining discovery and enterprise upon the sources of the Missouri. His communication is embraced in the appendix to this report.

In estimating the annual product of the precious metals from Montana, I adopted a rate, which did not seem entirely arbitrary, of doubling the mint deposits for the year ending June 30, 1866. These were $5,505,687 30, and on this basis the production of that year was assumed to be about $12,000,000. I am still of the opinion that this method of estimate is fair, and reasonably accurate in respect to gold, while, as to silver, so little is ever demanded for coinage that a much greater proportion passes into consumption from private assay. The deposits of gold from Montana at the mint, in Philadelphia, San Francisco, and Denver, and the assay office in New York, for the year ending June 30, 1867, amounted to $6,595,419 15. This amount doubled would be $13,190,838 30, or with an addition of the probable quantity of silver, it may be stated at $13,250,000.

Professor Keyes accepts a calculation, by N. P. Langford, esq., collector of internal revenue, based on population in 1867, which is reported at 24,000. Assuming an average population of 22,500 since 1864, and that the average cost of living is $750 per annum, these gentlemen infer that the population must have received from the mines the annual aggregate of $16,875,000. In the English mining colonies careful statements of the number engaged in gold mining are preserved; but the record in Australia, for 1867, only returns £80, or $400, per miner. There is probably no industry in the world so precarious, and in which there is so much time passed without productive results. Apply the Australian ratio to the entire average population of Montana, as above stated, and we have $9,000,000 per annum since 1864—a statement which is only $3,000,000 in excess of the estimate in my last report. The foregoing statement of $13,250,000, founded on the mint deposits of 1867, is more favorable to Montana than the estimate of Messrs. Langford and Keyes.

The area of the Territory is reported as 146,689$\frac{35}{100}$ square miles, equal to 93,881,184 acres—nearly the same as California, three times the area of New York, two and a half that of New England; and yet no greater proportion is claimed by local authorities as susceptible of cultivation than 1 acre in 30, or a total of 3,346,400 acres. Of course, a far greater surface will afford sustenance to domestic animals. The limit to agriculture, as in Colorado and New Mexico, is the possibility of irrigation.

Referring to the enclosed communication for further details, it is not deemed inappropriate to trace beyond the international frontier those physical features which have characterized the cordillera of the Sierra Madre from the 29th to the 49th parallel. These are attractively described by Father De Smet, the well known missionary, who, in 1845, crossed the mountains from the sources of the Columbia to the Bow river, or South fork of the Saskatchawan. Thence he continued northward, noticing coal on the Red Deer, a branch of the Bow river. Descending the valley of the Red Deer, he at length emerged upon what he described as "the vast plain, the ocean of prairies." He followed the general direction of the mountain chain to Edmonton House, in latitude 54°, whence he wrote in the following terms:

The entire region in the vicinity of the eastern chain of the Rocky mountains, serving as their base for 30 or 60 miles, is extremely fertile, abounding in forests, plains, prairies, lakes, streams, and mineral springs. The rivers and streams are innumerable, and on every side offer situations favorable for the construction of mills. The northern and southern branches of the Saskatchawan water the district I have traversed for a distance of about 300 miles. Forests of pines, cypress, thorn, poplar, and aspen trees, as well as others of different kinds, occupy a large portion of it, covering the declivities of the mountains and banks of the rivers. These originally take their rise in the highest chains, whence they issue in every direction like so many veins. The beds and sides of these rivers are pebbly, and their course rapid, but as they recede from the mountains they widen, and their currents lose something of their impetuosity. Their waters are usually very clear. The country would be capable of supporting a large population, and the soil is favorable for the production of wheat, barley, potatoes, and beans, which grow here as well as in the more southern countries.

As early as 1862, some American explorers washed from the bed of the north Saskatchawan river, at a distance of 200 miles from its extreme sources in the Rocky mountains, minute particles of gold, but with no return exceeding *one cent to the pan*, or $5 per day. In subsequent years the emigrants from Selkirk settlements, and a few American adventurers, obtained more satisfactory results, there being frequent instances of $10 as a daily average from bars or gulches nearer the mountains. As the Montana explorations have advanced towards the international frontier, each encampment proving more productive than its predecessors, the opinion has prevailed that the sources of the Saskatchawan would develop rich deposits of gold and silver, especially near the great centre of physical disturbance, where Mount Hooker reaches an elevation of 16,000 feet, and Mount Brown 15,700 feet above the sea, and from which the waters of the Saskatchawan, Peace, Frazer, and Columbia rivers diverge to three oceans. So prevalent is this belief in Montana that a sudden migration of thousands may at any moment be anticipated. American prospectors at the Kootanie mines have already passed the mountains on or beyond the boundary of 49°, and found rich washings, returning even $60 daily to the hand on the sources of the south Saskatchawan.

The limit of successful agriculture in the northern temperate zone should be carried considerably beyond the Saskatchawan valley, especially near the Rocky mountains. Sir Roderick Murchison, in an address before the London Geographical Society, represents this chain of mountains to be greatly depressed in high northern latitudes, and indeed several of the tributaries of the Mackenzie have their sources on the Pacific slope, and wind through the mountains before falling into the great Arctic river. The mountain valleys of the Peace and Liard rivers, latitude 56° to 60°, are thus influenced by the Pacific winds, and wheat and other cereals are successfully cultivated. Sir Alexander Mackenzie describes, under date of May 10, the exuberant verdure of the mountain valleys—trees about to blossom, and buffalo attended by their young. During an inquiry in 1858 by the English House of Commons into the situation of the territory of the Hudson's Bay Company, similar statements were elicited. Dr. Richard King, who accompanied an expedition in search of Sir John Ross, as "surgeon and naturalist," was asked what portion of the country visited by him was valuable for the purpose of settlement. In reply he described "as a very fertile valley a square piece of country," bounded on the south by Cumberland House, and by the Athabasca lake on the north. His own words are as follows:

The sources of the Athabasca and the sources of the Saskatchawan include an enormous area of country. It is, in fact, a vast piece of land surrounded by water. When I heard Dr. Livingston's description of that country, which he found in the interior of Africa, within the equator, it appeared to me to be precisely the kind of country which I am now describing. It is a rich soil, interspersed with well-wooded country, there being growth of every kind, and the whole vegetable kingdom alive.

When asked concerning mineral productions his reply was:

I do not know of any other mineral except limestone; limestone is apparent in all directions. * * * The birch, the beech, and the maple are in abundance, and there is every sort of fruit.

When questioned further, as to the growth of trees, Dr. King replied by a comparison "with the magnificent trees around Kensington Park in London." He described a farm near Cumberland House, under very successful cultivation—luxuriant wheat, potatoes, barley, pigs, cows, and horses.

Beyond the Athabasca district above described, the valley of the Mackenzie, parallel and adjacent to the northwestern trend of the Rocky mountains, is too Arctic in position and climate for successful agriculture, but will always possess interest to the geologist and mineralogist. Its course has been frequently followed by scientific observers, either employed by the Hudson's Bay Company, or commissioned by the English government for exploration of the Arctic coast. These observations are of interest, from their analogies to the formations previously noticed within the Territories of Montana, Colorado, and New Mexico, and because the extreme northern districts are only separated by a mountain chain from the comparatively unknown Territory of Alaska. The Saskatchawan basin is mostly silurian, but towards its western and northern borders coal measures are developed, which extend continuously to the Arctic ocean along the western bank of the Mackenzie. The preponderance of testimony is that the coal is lignite. Of this Mackenzie district, Sir John Richardson thus spoke in a communication published in the journal of the Geographical Society for 1845:

It is rich in minerals; inexhaustible coal-fields skirt the Rocky mountains through 12° of latitude; beds of coal crop out of the surface on various parts of the Arctic coast; veins of lead ore traverse the rocks of Coronation Gulf, and the Mackenzie river flows through a well-wooded tract, skirted by metalliferous ranges of mountains, and offers no obstruction to steam navigation for upwards of 1,200 miles.

DAKOTA.

Returning to the territory of the United States, the Black Hills on the western border of Dakota, between 44° and 45° latitude, and 103° and 105° longitude, will next receive notice. They are closely related to the Missouri and Yellowstone mines of Montana, and have been ascertained by the explorations of Lieutenant G. K. Warren in 1847, and of Captain W. F. Reynolds in 1859 and 1860, under direction of the United States topographical office, to be rich in gold and silver, as well as coal, iron, copper, and pine forests.

The area occupied by the Black Hills, as delineated on a map which accompanies Lieutenant Warren's report, is 6,000 square miles, or about the surface of Connecticut. Their bases are elevated from 2,500 to 3,500 feet, and the highest peaks are about 6,700 feet above the ocean level. The whole geological range of rocks, from the granite and metamorphosed azoic to the cretaceous formations of the surrounding plains, are developed by the upheaval of the mountain mass. Thus, at the junction of silurian rocks, gold becomes accessible, while the carboniferous strata bring coal measures within reach.

With the pacification of the Sioux Indians and the establishment of emigrant roads this district of Dakota would doubtless be the scene of great mining excitement, as the gold field of the Black Hills is accessible at a distance of 120 miles from the Missouri river.

MINNESOTA.

In 1865 attention was directed to discoveries of gold and silver northwest of Lake Superior, in the State of Minnesota. Lake Vermillion, an expansion of a stream of that name, is the centre of the district in question. The outline of this lake is very irregular. With a diameter of 30 miles, its surface is so studded with islands, its shores so broken with bays and headlands, that the entire coast line cannot be less than 200 miles in extent. In 1848 Dr. I. G. Norwood, of Owen's geological survey, passed from the mouth of the St. Louis river, at the western extremity of Lake Superior, to the sources of the Vermillion river, and, descending through the lake to the Rainy river, furnished a sketch of its natural features and mineral exposures. His statements are repeated so far as they record the usual indications of a gold formation.

Before entering Vermillion lake from the south, Dr. Norwood mentions a perpendicular fall of eight feet over "silicious slate, hard and gray, with minute grains of iron pyrites sparsely disseminated through it." This rock bears east and west, with thin seams of quartz between the laminæ, running in the line of bearing. There are also irregular patches of quartz, from 8 to 10 feet long and from 6 to 12 inches wide, which cross the strike at right angles. The river is broken by falls three-quarters of a mile above, or south of, Lake Vermillion.

The islands in the lake indicate very distinctly volcanic action, one of them being an extinct crater. The prevalent rocks are talcose slate, which Dr. Norwood describes as "eminently magnesian, thinly laminated, and traversed by numerous veins of quartz from an inch to five feet wide, some of which contain beautiful crystals of iron pyrites." He adds that, "from some indications noticed, other more valuable minerals will probably be found associated with it." A specimen obtained about midway of the lake is catalogued as "quartz of reddish brown color; crystalline, with yellow iron pyrites, crystallized as well as foliated disseminated through it."

These quartz veins were ascertained in 1865-'66 to be auriferous. A specimen weighing three pounds, containing copper pyrites, was forwarded by the governor of Minnesota to the mint in Philadelphia, and, upon assay, was found to contain $23 63 of gold and $4 42 of silver per ton of 2,000 pounds. The State geologist, Mr. H. H. Eames, reported an abundant supply of quartz equal in richness. Other assays in New York—in one instance by officers of the United States assay office—exhibited results from $10 to $35 per ton. Professor J. V. Z. Blaney, of Chicago, described a vein 10 feet in width, at the foot of a shaft of 50 feet, which was "indubitably gold-bearing," and added that "specimens taken from its central portion, as proven by assay, would be sufficient in California, Colorado, and other successful mining regions, to warrant further exploration." Washings of the drift near the veins opened have produced gold, but in limited quantities.

Difficulties of transportation; concurring with the general depression of mining interests in the basin of Lake Superior, have postponed the consummation of several enterprises for working the Vermillion mines; but a ton of quartz recently reduced at St. Paul is said to have yielded eight pounds of bullion, valued between $400 and $500. The question of their general productiveness remains to be determined.

CANADIAN MINES.

When, in 1862, gold was discovered upon the sources of the Saskatchawan, a newspaper at Selkirk settlement, the Norwester, published statements of the existence of gold between Lake Superior and Lake Winnipeg. Since the Vermillion discovery rumors of its extension into British America are prevalent, and suggest a probability that the mountain chain known to geographers as the Laurentian, which separates the waters of the St. Lawrence and its lakes from the tributaries of Hudson bay, may reveal to future explorers extensive deposits of gold and silver. The basin of the St. Lawrence, including the sandstones of Lake Superior, is a lower silurian formation; that of Hudson bay, granitic or primary, with many evidences in Minnesota and along the Canadian shore of Lake Superior of eruptive or igneous agencies.

Sir Rederick Murchison has frequently advanced the opinion that the productive gold districts of the world occur where the silurian, and perhaps the lower strata of Devonian, rocks are in contact with, or have been penetrated by, greenstones, porphyries, serpentine, granitic, and other rocks of the primary formation. Gold, especially when traced to its original matrix, is found to occur chiefly in veins or lodes of quartz rising from beneath and cutting through the secondary strata or beds of which the surface was previously composed. These conditions are observed in the Vermillion district, and Professor Owen, as early as 1850, traced in this locality of Minnesota, and northeastwardly along the north shore of Lake Superior, in Canada, what he denominated a "great plutonic chain," and the "main axis of dislocation," from which silurian sandstones extend southwardly through Wisconsin and Minnesota, while on the north the streams which are turned towards Hudson bay traverse a region exclusively granitic or primary. If in Minnesota an auriferous belt has marked this line of junction, we may with reason anticipate its extension eastwardly into Canada and northwestwardly towards Lake Winnipeg. Indeed, as English explorers trace this con tact of primary and silurian formations along the basins of Lakes Slave and Athabasca and the channel of the Mackenzie to the Arctic ocean, it becomes an interesting problem for future solution whether the auriferous deposits of British Columbia and Saskatchawan may not be extended, with various degrees of productiveness, along the crest which separates the waters of the Gulfs of Mexico and St. Lawrence from those of the Arctic ocean and Hudson bay, quite as the discoveries of this century now follow the Ural mines eastward, through Siberia, to the Pacific.

The intrusion of granitic rocks is not confined in Minnesota to the northeastern angle of the State. It has been traced southwestwardly, near Sauk rapids, upon the Upper Minnesota, and even to the northwestern boundary of Iowa, in a wedge-like shape, although covered in most places by the mass of drift which constitutes so large a portion of the surface of Minnesota. A similar granitic cape, with its associated minerals, may be the explanation of the alleged gold deposits in the township of Madoc, near Kingston, in Canada West.

In 1867 occurred an important discovery of native silver near Fort William, on Thunder bay of Lake Superior, almost at the western limit of Canada. Miners from Ontonagon have visited the locality and returned with specimens of native silver, lead, copper ore, and mundic. The native silver is principally disseminated in the vein matrix, much like stamp copper, and its weight runs from 1 to 10 per cent. of the rock. The lead is also highly charged with silver ore. Although many claims have been secured, yet only two shafts have been sunk. From these, which have reached a depth of 30 to 40 feet, a considerable amount of ore has been taken, consisting of native silver, black sulphuret of silver, argentiferous galena, and leaf silver through the spar. These shafts are upon one lode, which is fully 20 feet in width, having an east and west bearing, with dip to the north. The sheet of mineral and metal is about four inches in thickness, interspersed through the spar and quartz and mingled with hornblende. The yield of the working ores, from practical assay, is stated to be at the rate of $700 per ton. If the current information in regard to these silver mines at Fort William is confirmed, they will soon be the centre of great mining excitement.

A discovery of gold on the north shore of Lake Superior, in the region of Black bay, between Thunder bay and the river Neepigon, is communicated by Professor E. J. Chapman to the Toronto Globe. He represents that repeated assays have yielded amounts of gold varying per ton from 15 to 19 pennyweights, the mean being 17 pennyweights 12 grains, with about two ounces of silver—results obtained from surface specimens only, and showing a value of nearly $21 per ton, irrespective of considerable amounts of copper and lead. The enclosing rock is described as silurian.

The discoveries in the Madoc district, near Belleville, in Canada West, or Ontario, have been extended, geographically, during the past year, and reduction works by several responsible companies are nearly completed. Much mystery attends the degree of success by the different claims now in course of development, but there is good reason to believe that next summer's operations will vindicate the wisdom of the very considerable investments which have been made.

The latest and most reliable statement in regard to the Madoc mines is presented by the gold inspector of the Quinte mining district, for the month of January, 1868, from which it appears that the reduction of ores by working process from 45 district localities, 19 yielded gold in paying quantities, 14 in smaller quantities, and 12 showed blank. The highest returns were $40 and $62 per ton. Of the mines from which samples have hitherto been sent to the two reducing establishments, now in operation, 42 per cent. will pay to work from the first, 34 per cent. are worthy of further trial, and only 26 per cent. show no appreciable result. The greatest depth of excavation yet reached is 70 feet.

The auriferous alluvians of Lower Canada cover an extended region estimated by the geological commission to embrace 10,000 square miles. The gravels, through which the gold is very irregularly distributed, are generally covered by a layer of vegetable earth and often by a bed of clay. They repose in part upon metamorphic lower silurian rocks consisting of schists, generally talcose, micaceous or chloritic, associated with diorites and serpentines. But to the southward these lower silurian strata are unconformably overlaid by others of upper silurian age, which are also covered by gold-bearing alluvians. These upper rocks consist of argillaceous schists, with sandstones and limestones all more or less altered. The rocks of these two formations, but especially of the upper silurian, are traversed by numerous veins of quartz running in the direction of the stratification, or between northeast and east. Mr. A. Michel, from whom these particulars are obtained, compares these Canadian deposits with the auriferous sands of the Ural or Altai mountains, in Siberia, which are rarely found reposing on granitic or syenitic rocks, but almost always on schistose rocks in the vicinity of diorites and serpentines, which has led the Russian mining engineers to consider the gold as having "its principal source in the ferruginous quartz of the metamorphic schists, and in the vicinity of the serpentines and diorites."

These mines are called Chaudiere, as upon that tributary of the St. Lawrence and its branches, in the Seignory of Vaudreuil, the principal placers have been discovered, and there, also, the only quartz lodes have been successfully worked. Alluvial mining is no longer prosecuted, although favorable reports have been circulated since 1851, and Mr. T. Sterry Hunt, of the Canadian geological survey, claims that the river banks would richly repay the use of hydraulic methods. Assuming that the cost in Canada of washing gravel by this method would be one-fourth as much as in California, or five cents the cubic yard, he adds that the auriferous alluvian over an acre at the forks of the Du Loup and Chaudiere yielded, during the workings in 1851–'52, at the rate of one and thirty-eight hundredths grain of gold to the cubic foot, which is equal to 37 grains to the cubic yard. At the ordinary fineness of the alluvial gold of the Chaudiere region, the value of this would be $1 33 as the yield of a cubic yard of gravel. The alluvial gold of this district is not confined to the gravel of river channels, nor to alluvial flats, but is found in gravels high above the river beds, to which the hydraulic method might be applied with advantage even though the proportion of gold was much less than near the Du Loup.

Prof. Hunt gives the results of 31 assays of gold-bearing rock, from 12 different localities. Of these assays 18 gave no trace of gold, while the remaining 13 gave the following returns: 1. Of five assays four gave an average of only 6 dwts., 13 grains of gold = $6 76, while the fifth, in which a large scale of gold was seen in sifting and was added to the assay, yielded at the rate of 4 ounces, 18 dwts., = $101 29; the average of the five assays being $25 66 per ton. 2. From another locality in the Seignory of Vaudreuil, four assays gave a mean of 4 dwts., 21 grains, = $5 03; and that of two others, in which a scale of gold was seen and ground up with the powder, gave 3 ounces, 2 dwts., = $64 07, the average of the six assays being $24 71 to the ton. 3. Two Vaudreuil assays gave a mean of 14 dwts., 16 grains, = $15 15. 4. Two assays from another district, Liniere, gave a mean of 6 dwts., 13 grains, = $6 76 to the ton.

This record does not place the success of quartz mining beyond all contingency; but a well organized company is now engaged in experiments which will determine the question during 1868.

NOVA SCOTIA.

There is no district on this continent, not excepting the Grass Valley mines of California, where the reduction of auriferous quartz has been more successful than in Nova Scotia. Two important elements concur in this result—the cheapness of commodities under light taxation, and the great facilities of access from the sea, and by good roads.

Hon. P. S. Hamilton, commissioner of mines at Halifax, has favored me with an elaborate communication upon the gold mines of Nova Scotia, including some notice of the coal measures, which is given in the appendix. The production of gold during 1867 amounted to $517,140.

THE ALLEGHANY GOLD FIELDS.

The Appalachian chain takes its origin in Canada, southeast of the St. Lawrence, and forms a broad belt of mountain ridges extending in a southwesterly direction to Alabama. The entire length of the chain is about 1,300 miles ; its breadth is variable, gradually expanding towards its centre, and contracting at each extremity. The most striking feature of this mountain system is the fact that it is made up of a series of parallel ridges, very numerous, especially in Pennsylvania and Virginia, no one of which can be considered as being the main or central chain to which the others are subordinate, but the whole forming a system of flexures which gradually open out from the southeast to the northwest, as has been made evident from the results of the geological surveys of Pennsylvania and Virginia, under the direction of Professors H. D. and W. B. Rodgers. Along the southeastern edge of this great Appalachian system is a relatively narrow, undulating range, known under different names in the different States. In Vermont it is called the Green mountains ; in New York, the Highlands ; in Pennsylvania, the South mountains ; in Virginia, the Blue Ridge ; in North Carolina, the Smoky mountains. The rocks of this belt, which has a width of 10 or 15 miles, are of the lower palæozoic age, but highly metamorphosed, and, for the most part, having their organic remains entirely obliterated. Still further to the southeast lies the great auriferous belt, nearly parallel with the Blue Ridge, and not easily separated from it in geological age, either lithologically or by palæontological characters. The central axis of this belt has a direction in Virginia of about north 32° east ; towards the north it assumes a more nearly north and south direction, and to the south it approaches an east and west line. Its width, where most developed, does not exceed 70 miles. This is about its extent on the borders of North and South Carolina. In Virginia it does not exceed 15 miles. Starting from Georgia and proceeding northward, we find it developed in the following counties: In Georgia, in Carroll, Cobb, Cherokee, Lumpkin, and Habersham counties ; in South Carolina, through the whole northwestern corner of the State, especially in the following districts : Abbeville, Pickens, Spartanburg, Union, York, Lancaster ; in North Carolina, in Mecklenburg, Rutherford, Cabarrus, Rowan, Davidson, Guilford, and Rockingham ; thence through Virginia, in Pittsylvania, Campbell, Buckingham, Fluvanna, Louisa, Spottsylvania, Orange, Culpeper, Fauquier ; in Maryland, Montgomery county. Beyond Maryland, to the north, the indications become fainter, and consist only in a few scattered lumps or fine scales occasionally picked up, until we reach Canada, where there is a considerable extent proved to be auriferous.

Throughout this whole extent the auriferous belt presents rocks of nearly the same character ; they are slates of every variety intermixed with bands of a granite and syenitic character. The predominating kind of slate is talcose, passing into chloritic and argillaceous. The prevailing dip is to the east at a very high angle. In Virginia they stand nearly vertical.*

Since the California discovery of 1848 little attention has been given to alluvial mining in Virginia, the Carolinas, and Georgia, and until recently capitalists have acquiesced in the opinion so confidently expressed by Sir Roderick Murchison, in " Siluria " and other publications, that, notwithstanding numerous filaments and traces of gold near their surface, the Alleghany vein-stones held no body of ore downwards which would warrant deep quartz mining. At present, with 20 years' experience in gold mining ; with the testimony of miners in Colorado, that a lode apparently closed by cap-rock can be recovered with increased richness at a lower depth ; with other analogies, however imperfect, from the successful treatment of pyritous ores in Nova Scotia ; and with the earnest application of inventive minds to new and improved processes of desulphurization, it is evident that the working of the southern mines will be resumed,

---

* Whitney's Metallic Wealth of the United States.

perhaps with the encouragement of a scientific survey under the auspices of the general government.

The deposits of gold at the United States mint and its branches between 1804 and 1836, from the States traversed by the Appalachian gold-field, are reported as follows:

Virginia	$1,570,182 82
North Carolina	9,278,627 67
South Carolina	1,353,663 98
Georgia	6,971,681 50
Alabama	201,734 63
	19,375,890 80

If we admit that an equal quantity passed into manufactures or foreign commerce without deposit for coinage, the aggregate production would be about $40,000,000, of which fully three-fourths, or $30,000,000, was mined between 1828 and 1848.

It might be expected that during the year ending June 30, 1867, the productions of the southern mines would reach results as considerable as at any former period. The United States mint and branches report the deposits of that fiscal year from the Alleghany States as follows:

Alabama	$437 30
Georgia	28,758 20
South Carolina	1,200 54
North Carolina	66,305 62
Virginia	10,205 90
	106,907 56

It was my purpose to give in detail the organizations for gold mining in the south Atlantic States, with practical results, but so far the attention of parties interested has been so exclusively occupied in acquiring titles and preparing for actual operations, that it seems inexpedient at this time to attempt such a detailed statement. Referring, therefore, to my preliminary report for a review of the geological and mineralogical features of the region in question, I repeat the following general observations:

1. There is yet much room for the vigorous and intelligent prosecution of alluvial mining; especially in Georgia, where the country is abrupt and nature has subjected the auriferous rocks to much dislocation and atmospheric exposure, not only the beds of the rivers, but the adjacent detritus of their valleys, will unquestionably give large returns to the new and powerful methods for washing ponderous masses of earth. It is understood that companies are now organized who propose to introduce these hydraulic appliances upon the Chestatee and other tributaries of the Chattahoochee river.

2. There is abundant evidence, too, that the upper portions of auriferous lodes have been in a remarkable degree desulphurized, and may be worked to a considerable depth with great advantage before the intrusion of what is called "cap" in Colorado, or before the main body of the vein becomes obstinately pyritiferous. Surface quartz mining, if the phrase is admissible, will warrant considerable investments whatever subsequent experience shall demonstrate in regard to the refractory sulphurets. It may be admitted that hitherto a quartz so modified in chemical constitution as to be honey-combed, having become cellular and brittle from the decomposition of pyrites, with the gold set free from its matrix, is the only material which it is profitable to reduce. But the testimony is ample that immense quantities of ore in this favorable situation are accessible in the Allegheny gold district.

3. There are no grounds for the opinion that the auriferous lodes, strongly marked as they are by native sulphurets, will not prove true fissure veins,

improving in quantity and quality with their depth. Professor Frederick Overman, in a work entitled "Practical Mineralogy," published in 1851, claims that the pyritous veins of Virginia and other south Atlantic States will be more sure and lasting than the gold-bearing localities of California. If the lower beds of Colorado mines can be raised and reduced with profit, deep sinking will be equally successful in the Carolinas.

METALLURGICAL TREATMENT.

The process of amalgamation still generally prevails in the mining districts enumerated. It consists in reducing auriferous rock to a fine powder by means of stamps, arrastras, Chilian mills, or other mechanical contrivance, and subjecting it to a continuous agitation with mercury, with water enough to give a pasty consistency to the mass, the object being to expose as fully as possible the fine particles of gold and silver to the attractive power of the mercury, with which they form an *amalgam* easily separable by subsidence in the lighter pulp of earthy matter of which the ore consists. The amalgam thus obtained on being subjected to moderate heat in an iron retort gives up its mercury, which passes over in vapor and is condensed again in another vessel, the metal being left in the retort.

In the case of pyritic ores, however, it is found that the process of amalgamation is seriously retarded by the impurities with which the gold and silver are associated. Probably the ores of Colorado do not yield by simple amalgamation an average of 20 per cent. of their assay value. A previous process of desulphurization is therefore indispensable, and how best to accomplish this is the problem which has occupied the attention of metallurgists for many years. Many methods have been advised, the majority of which being merely empirical have had but an ephemeral reputation.

The opinion is widely prevalent that smelting—the attack of gold or silver bearing ores by fire—will be the final and indispensable expedient for separating the precious metals from its matrix. If smelting works on a large scale could be established in all the mining Territories, there would doubtless ensue a subdivision of labor in the business of mining gold and silver, as is now the case in iron mining. The miner would limit his efforts to raising ore from the mine, and the smelting furnace would afford a market where the ore might command its price, which would be better for all parties than the method hitherto pursued, of raising and reducing ores under one administration.

But at present there are two great obstacles to such a development of mining in the Rocky mountain districts, and perhaps elsewhere: excessive prices of machinery, chemicals, and utensils, resulting in a great degree from the high rates of taxation, external and internal; and the cost of transportation west of the Missouri river. The former is of universal application; the latter has special reference to the interior districts of New Mexico, Colorado, and Montana, as well as other western Territories. Except for these causes of obstruction the gold and silver product of the United States could be readily doubled. They will be considered with some fulness of illustration.

TAXATION.

It will be instructive in this connection to compare the taxation of Victoria, the leading province of Australia, and the United States, premising that 10 per cent. in addition should be added to the Victoria rates, to express the difference of freights, interest, and insurance, over the shorter communication between Europe and the United States. Tables have been compiled from the American tariff of 1867, and the latest revision of the Victoria tariff, and are presented in the appendix No. V. The tariff of Victoria has been recently advanced beyond the average of the other Australian colonies.

The taxation of Nova Scotia has not hitherto exceeded an average on the dutiable list of 10 per cent., although, as an incident of confederation with Canada, it has been recently raised to 20 per centum.

Far the largest portion of the importations in Victoria are charged with a duty of five per centum, while the average duties on the whole bulk of imports, under the tariff of the United States, has been computed by the special commissioner of revenue at 42.71 per cent.

In all the gold districts of the world, the opportunities of placer mining induce a high price of labor; and hence the great necessity that government shall impose the lowest rates of taxation consistent with its necessities upon machinery and other materials or utensils, which experience has proved indispensable to the exploration of mines. At present the burden inseparable from an ill-adjusted revenue system is a grave obstacle to the increase of our supply of the precious metals.

TRANSPORTATION.

A ton of ore in California producing $10 is remunerative of capital and labor employed; and in Canada, Nova Scotia, and the southern States it is profitable to reduce auriferous or argentiferous rock where the average yield is $8 per ton. Yet, in the mining Territories of the Rocky mountains, on account mainly of the cost of transportation, a lode must yield $25 average per ton to warrant its occupation and improvement.

Some statements from the official records of the quartermasters' bureau of the War Department will illustrate the oppressive freights now imposed on the people of the remote interior by the necessity of wagon transportation. In 1865 the cost of transportation of a pound of corn, hay, clothing, subsistence, lumber, or any other necessary, from Fort Leavenworth to—

	Cents.
Fort Riley was	2.46
Fort Union, the depot for New Mexico	14.35
Santa Fé, New Mexico	16.85
Fort Kearney	6.44
Fort Laramie	14.10
Denver City, Colorado	15.43
Salt Lake City, Utah	27.84

The cost of a bushel of corn purchased at Fort Leavenworth and delivered at each of these points was as follows:

Fort Riley	$2 79
Fort Union	9 44
Santa Fé	10 84
Fort Kearney	5 03
Fort Laramie	9 26
Denver City	10 05
Great Salt Lake City	17 00

To the last point none was sent.

During the fiscal year ending June 30, 1863, the Quartermaster General estimated the cost of transportation of military stores westward across the plains as follows:

1. Northern and western route:		
To Utah and posts on that route		$1,524,119 00
2. Southwestern route:		
To Fort Union, New Mexico, and posts on that route	$1,301,400	
To posts in the interior of New Mexico	138,178	
		1,439,578 00
Cost of the transportation of grain on above routes, where the grain was delivered by contractors, and the transportation entered into the price paid the same year:		
1. Utah route	$2,526,727 68	
2. New Mexico route	697,101 69	
		3,223,829 37
Cost of transportation of military stores across the plains same year by government trains:		
1. Utah route	$34,600	
2. New Mexico route	166,730	
		201,330 00
Total by contract and government trains		6,388,856 37

Under date of April 18, 1866, General M. C. Meigs, Quartermaster General, furnished the following unofficial statement:

The distances to the northwest are great; the interior and local transportation as costly. The use of the Missouri river, however, will enable the government to place a large part of its supplies upon the upper waters of that river, by taking advantage of the summer rise, and thus the extent of land transportation will be reduced; but, until the Missouri valley itself is settled, the navigation will continue to be slow and perilous. Steamers are now obliged to stop from day to day to cut green cottonwood or drift-wood upon the banks, and a trip to the upper Missouri is a season's work. Many boats are wrecked; some are caught by the falling waters and compelled to winter on the upper river. Insurance to Fort Benton, the head of navigation, costs 20 per cent.; and the government has this year been obliged to engage freight from St. Louis to-Forts Berthold and Union, old trading posts now about to be occupied by troops as military posts, at $5 per 100 pounds, or $100 per ton. Fort Union is, in a direct line, 330 miles below Fort Benton; by the river the distance is probably one-half greater. From Fort Union the supply of the troops and posts throughout Montana and the districts supplied from the east will be by wagon trains. On the well-travelled and well-guarded routes of the central and southwestern overland trails the cost of this transportation by contract last year averaged 45 cents per ton per mile. The contracts for the present year are at much lower rates, but in the remote districts of the northwest such favorable rates cannot be expected as yet. The distance from St. Louis to Fort Benton by river is estimated at 3,450 miles by river men. The cost of transportation of freight to that point is $350 to $400 per ton. From St. Louis to Helena, a town of 4,000 inhabitants, which has sprung into being in Montana within the past year, the estimated cost of transportation of freight by the river and wagon trail is $500 to $600 per ton.

Within the last two years the construction of the Union Pacific railroad has contributed to the reduction of the aggregates paid for freight, although the wagon rates are not materially diminished. In 1866 the rates from the Missouri river to northern Colorado, Nebraska, Dakota, Idaho, and Utah were $1 45; to southern Colorado, Kansas, and New Mexico, $1 38, with an addition from Fort Union, in New Mexico, to posts in that Territory, in Arizona, and western Texas, of $1 79 per 100 pounds per 100 miles. The total number of pounds transported was 81,489,321, or 40,774.10 tons, at a cost of $3,314,495.

A prominent citizen of Montana authorizes the following statements of the amount paid annually by the government of the United States and by the people of Montana for transportation. During 1867 there were 40 arrivals of steamers by the Missouri river, averaging 150 tons of freight, an aggregate of 6,000 tons. An equal quantity was delivered by wagons from the west and south. He estimates that the average charges for freight and insurance were 25 cents per pound, which, on 12,000 tons, would be not less than $6,000,000. If the population of Montana is 30,000, this would be $200 per capita; if the population is 60,000, as sometimes claimed, $100 per capita. A merchant is deprived for seven months of the year of the use of his capital—a very considerable loss of interest. In addition, the unavoidable expenses of travel, incident to the business of the country, is an immense tax. A trip to the eastern cities, or to the Pacific coast, requires a direct expenditure of $1,000. It is estimated that 20 such journeys weekly are already incident to the intercourse of the people with the business centres of the country; and if so, another million must be added to the account of transportation expenses. The wonder is, notwithstanding the richness and productiveness of the Montana mines, that such a burden can be borne, while the effect upon prices can be readily conceived.

This statement of the amounts paid for transportation in Montana will not seem improbable when it is remembered that $13,000,000 in gold was paid in 1863 for transportation eastward from San Francisco to the State of Nevada and Territories east of the Sierra Nevada.

The progress of population under these oppressive conditions in the mining States and Territories of the west, gives an assurance that the construction of an adequate railway system from the Mississippi river to the Pacific coast would be attended with such an extension of settlements as would justify the immediate reduction of rates of transportation to one-third of those now prevailing. A large saving to the government upon its unavoidable movement of men and supplies would also follow.

When in 1853 the initiative of Pacific railroad exploration was presented to the United States Senate, resulting in a congressional appropriation of $150,000 for the purpose, attention was directed to three routes—the northern, the central, and the southern. Legislation has followed in behalf of one, the central, not so much from any demonstration of greater feasibility, but because the mineral discoveries of the interior, followed by population, suggested the selection. The same causes are now active on the two other routes. Discoveries, not only of gold and silver, but of coal, iron, lead, and salt, diversify the map of the Rocky Mountain region everywhere within our boundaries; and an emigration from the Pacific coast meets the Atlantic column even upon the great plains, which are drained by the Missouri, the Platte, and the Rio Grande.

The necessity of more than one route between the Mississippi States and the Pacific coast will appear from an enumeration of the railroad lines which are indispensable to the commerce between the Atlantic and interior States. These are seven well-defined thoroughfares: 1. From Portland, by the Grand Trunk to Detroit, and thence with a traverse of the State and lake of Michigan to Milwaukee and La Crosse. 2. By the New York Central, the Great Western, of Canada, and the Chicago and Northwestern railroad, to Prairie du Chien. 3. By the New York and Erie, the lines of Ohio and Indiana south of the great lakes, and the Illinois Central, to Galena. 4. The Pennsylvania Central and its western connections to Rock Island. 5. The Baltimore and Ohio, by way of Cincinnati to St. Louis. 6. From Richmond, through the Cumberland valley to Memphis. 7. From Charleston and Savannah, traversing the States of Georgia, Alabama, and Mississippi, to Vicksburg and New Orleans. All these highways are thronged and prosperous, and, with the wonderful impulse to colonization and commerce induced by mining investments, the period seems to have arrived when a wise statesmanship is fully justified in proposing a westward extension of continental communications upon the following lines:

First. Through the southern tier of States, on or near the parallel of 35°, which is central to the region of cotton, the sugar cane, and the vine, and which will be supported by the populations of Louisiana, Arkansas, Neosho, (or the territory occupied by the Cherokee and Choctaw Indians,) Texas, New Mexico, Arizona, Sonora, and southern California. This may be called the gulf route from its relations to the gulfs of Mexico and California.

Second. The central, which is now in course of construction on the average latitude of 40°, with its present prestige and aid from the federal government; the speedy construction of this road may be anticipated in 1870. If in operation at the present moment the road would be financially successful. All the resources of Kansas, Nebraska, Colorado, Utah, Nevada, and, in a great degree, of Missouri and California, are pledged to such a result.

Third. The lake route, hitherto designated in congressional debates as the northern Pacific route, connecting the western coast of the great lakes and the navigable channel of the Columbia river by the most direct and feasible communication with which the Territories and future States of Dakota, Montana, Idaho, and Washington, as well as the States of Minnesota and Oregon, are identified.

A few illustrations will be given of the possibilities of State aid in behalf of such improvements without involving permanent financial burdens.

When, 10 years ago, India was exhausted, by a mutiny of the native population, and its suppression after a desperate struggle, a railway system, penetrating the whole of the peninsula of Hindostan, was deemed essential to its military occupation, and the government of India offered a guarantee of five per cent. on the stock required to construct and equip not less than 5,000 miles of railroad. The total amount of capital raised under this guarantee to April 1,

1867, was £67,254,802; but of this amount the government liability has already ceased upon £42,584,649, the roads constructed with that sum not only paying dividends of five per cent. to the stockholders, but a surplus for reimbursement of previous advances by government. Four thousand miles of railroad have thus been assured to India, and so wisely are the securities adjusted that this immense boon to the people will not be attended by permanent burdens to the finances of the province. With the aid of these communications India hopes to rival the United States in the production of cotton.

The province of Victoria, in Australia, has incurred a debt of £10,000,000 in the construction of railways, from which the total gross revenues in the year 1865 amounted to £717,162, almost sufficient, after the deduction of current expenses, to discharge an interest of six per centum on their cost of construction. The reduction of the rates of transportation from Melbourne to the gold districts of Ballarat and Bendigo, is far greater than we have ventured to anticipate from the construction of railroads through the western Territories of the United States.

In Belgium the state is a great railway proprietor, and the state railway is the largest source of national revenue. It was the first work of the kind ever undertaken by a government, or on so grand a scale by any proprietary. The act by which it was decreed passed in 1834, and in 1835 the line was open from Brussels to Malines. In 1844 the entire length—560 kilometres—was completed. It produced to the State a gross revenue in 1863 of 31,750,000 francs, or £1,270,000, and a net revenue of 16,000,000 francs, or £640,000. Other lines have been leased by the state, and there are altogether open 1,906 kilometres, equal to 1,191 English miles; of which 748 kilometres, or 467 English miles, are in the hands of the state, and the residue worked by companies. It is calculated that in the year 1884 the net revenue will amount to 24,000,000 francs, or £960,000, per annum, or enough to pay the then reduced (through the sinking fund) interest of the national debt. As each conceded railway lapses gratuitously to the state in 90 years from the period of its construction, the entire system will, by the efflux of time, become national property.

The growth of the railway system of France dates from the year 1840, previous to which there were but few lines in France. For a time the idea was entertained of making all the railways which were to be built state property, but in the end it was determined and settled by the law of June 11, 1842—modified in 1858, 1859, and 1863—that the work should be left to private companies, superintended, however, and, if necessary, assisted in their operations by the State. The French railways at present are almost entirely (the exception being to the amount of less than 200 miles) in the hands of six great companies. The length of lines held by each of these companies on January 1, 1867, was as follows: Paris, Lyons, and Mediterranean, 1,994¾ miles; Eastern of France, 1,559¾ miles; Orleans, 1,829¾ miles; Western of France, 1,051¼ miles; Northern of France, 728½ miles, and Southern of France, 827½ miles. The six systems combined had thus, in 1867, an aggregate of 7,989⅝ miles in operation. The conventions agreed on between the government and the railway companies in the years 1858, 1859, and 1863 were carried into effect on January 1, 1865. By these conventions the government guarantees 4 per cent. interest and 65c. for a sinking fund; altogether, 4f. 65c. per cent. on the capital expended in the construction of a certain number of lines classed under the collective title of new work, (nouveau reseau.) The sum to be expended by the six great companies was estimated at 7,100,000,000 francs, and the works executed and grants made by the government at 1,640,000,000 francs, being in round numbers about nine milliards of francs, of which there remain only about 2,500,000,000 francs to be expended. It is expected that in the course of about half a century the companies will be able to divide their surplus receipts with the government, while at the expiration of the 99 years' leases granted to the railway companies the railways will become the property of the State, which will gratuitously receive the total amount of the receipts, which, if estimated at only from 350,000,000 to 400,000,000 francs, will pay the full amount of the interest on the national debt.

Of the Prussian railways six lines (the most important that from Frankfort-on-the-Odor to Konigsburg and the Russian frontier, 101 German miles long) are State property; seven others are under government control, having been partly constructed by State loans or subventions; and the rest (about two-thirds of the whole) in the hands of private companies. The State railways form an important source of public revenue. In the financial estimates for the year 1865 the general receipts of the state railways were stated at 14,197,000 thalers, and the expenditure at 7,386,300 thalers, showing a surplus of 6,360,700 thalers, of which latter the sum of 467,700 thalers was derived from the Lower Silesian railway, 4,000 thalers from the Berlin junction, 566,600 thalers from the Eastern, 294,500 thalers from the Westphalian, and 256,700 thalers from the Saarbruck. From the above surplus of 6,360,700 thalers the sum of 4,889,257 thalers was deducted to pay off loans and debts contracted for railway purposes, leaving a net balance of 1,471,443 thalers towards defraying the general expenses of the State.

The total length of railways in the former kingdom of Hanover amounted to 550 English miles in 1863. The gross receipts of the same in the year ending July 1, 1863, was £838,085, and the net revenue £419,754. The whole of these lines are State property.

The public debt of Wurtemburg has more than doubled within the last 20 years, owing to the establishment of the railway lines of the kingdom, the whole of which, without exception, are State property. According to an official return published June 30, 1860, there had been expended at that period, both for railways and steamers, a sum of 42,824,956 florins, or £3,568,746. As the capital was borrowed at from 3½ to 4½ per cent., and the net incomes of the railways, all expenses deducted, and making allowance for wear and tear, amounted to between six and seven per cent., the investment so made contributed considerably towards lightening the burdens of the tax-payers. The length of the lines given to the traffic amounted on October 15, 1861, to 266 English miles; but this did not complete the whole network of railways which is expected to be finished by the end of 1867.

All the railways of Baden are property of the State, giving a dividend on the capital expended of above six per cent. The accounts of the income and expenditure of the State railways, as well as the post office and steam navigation on the Lake of Constance, are not entered in the general budget, but form a special fund.

Further illustrations of the railroad policy of Spain, Austria, and Russia might be adduced, showing the advantages of a comprehensive and well-guarded system, by which the credit of the state is in the first instance made available for the exigencies of construction, and, with the great resulting benefits to the people, soon becomes capitalized to the relief of the public treasury. There is no finer opportunity for an enlightened statesmanship than to utilize these European precedents in the interest of a national system of railways west of the Missouri river, but the province of this report will hardly admit of more than a bare suggestion, waiving advocacy or details.*

TREASURE PRODUCT OF THE WORLD.

The year 1848, or the epoch of the gold discovery in California, may be selected for a general statement of the amount of precious metals available for

---

* The statistics of European railways are compiled from a London publication, "The Statesman's Year Book for 1868," by Frederick Martin.

the uses of currency and the arts. M. Chevalier estimates the amount as $8,500,000,000, of which one-third was gold. An eminent English authority, Mr. M. W. Newmarch, states the probable quantity held in Europe and America at that date to be $6,800,000,000, with a similar proportion of silver to gold. The difference between these estimates, or $1,700,000,000, may be accepted as a moderate statement of the quantities of gold and silver in those countries of Asia and elsewhere which have not been closely related to European and American commerce.

Since 1848 the average production of the world has amounted to $200,000,000, but the proportions of gold and silver have been reversed; fully two-thirds of the aggregate being gold. The treasure product of 1867 is slightly increased above this average, and may be briefly stated as follows:

	Gold.	Silver.	Total.
United States	$60,000,000	$15,000,000	$75,000,000
Mexico and South America	5,000,000	35,000,000	40,000,000
Australia	60,000,000	1,000,000	61,000,000
British America	5,000,000	500,000	5,500,000
Russia	15,000,000	1,500,000	16,500,000
Elsewhere	25,000,000	2,000,000	27,000,000
Total	170,000,000	55,000,000	225,000,000

A brief analysis of the reasons for this estimate will be given.

The commissioner upon the mineral statistics of the Pacific slope has presented, in his general communication to the department, sufficient details of the treasure product of the United States, and the causes of its decline in comparison with former years.

In regard to Mexico and South America, Humboldt estimated the annual produce of the mines of Spanish America at the beginning of the present century to be $43,500,000. This amount was increased from 1800 to 1809, fully reaching $50,000,000 per annum, but in the last-mentioned year the contest began which terminated in the dissolution of the connection between Spain and her American colonies. The convulsions and insecurity arising out of this struggle, the proscription of the old Spanish families to whom the mines principally belonged, who repaired with the wrecks of their fortunes, some to Cuba, some to Spain, and some to Bordeaux and the south of France, caused the abandonment of several of the mines and an extraordinary falling off in the amount of their produce. There are no means of estimating the precise extent of this decline, but, according to Jacob, who collected and compared the existing information on the subject, the total average produce of the American mines, inclusive of Brazil, during the 20 years ending with 1829 may be estimated at $20,000,000 a year, being less than half their produce at the beginning of the century.

The discovery of new mines, and the greater cheapness and more abundant supplies of quicksilver obtained from California, have conspired, with other causes, to increase the produce of the South American mines, until, in 1867, they have nearly reached the productiveness of 1800; and the above estimate of their produce may be distributed as follows :

Mexico	$23,000,000
Peru	6,000,000
Bolivia	2,000,000
Chili	5,000,000
Other parts	4,000,000
	40,000,000

The latest and most satisfactory authority upon the production of Australia consists of a memorial from representatives of the different colonies to the home government upon postal communications between Australia and the mother country, dated April 1, 1867, in which occurs a table of exports of the associated colonies during 1865, giving the item of gold as follows :

Victoria	£6,190,317
New South Wales	2,647,658
New Zealand	2,226,474
Queensland	101,352
Total	11,165,811

It is a remarkable fact that the single colony of Victoria produced, in 1852, a gross amount of £14,866,799, far exceeding the entire aggregate from all the Australian colonies at this time. New South Wales, in 1852, produced £3,000,000 also in excess of the present productions of that colony. New Zealand has recently gone far to supply the deficiencies, and other gold fields are in course of discovery, and hence the foregoing aggregate of $61,000,000, adding to the exports of the different colonies about $6,000,000, may be accepted as a probable statement of the Australian treasure product.

The annual production of Russia was stated, in 1858, by J. R. McCulloch, in a treatise upon the precious metals, to be 87,500,000 francs, or £3,500,000, slightly exceeding the foregoing estimate. Late discoveries of placer mines upon the Amoor, in eastern Siberia, will probably lead, during 1868, to large additions to the annual average hitherto prevailing.

Mr. McCulloch estimated the total supply of gold and silver in 1858 as follows :

America, excluding California	$45,000,000
Asiatic Russia	17,500,000
Europe	7,750,000
California	70,000,000
Australia	55,000,000
	195,250,000

If to this amount we add $25,000,000, representing the production of Japan, China, India, Polynesia, and Africa, the total amount will be $220,250,000.

Great uncertainty attends the question of the probable production of the precious metals in the countries last named, described by M. Chevalier as "countries imperfectly accessible to the commerce of the world." The French economist does not materially differ from the estimates of McCulloch in regard to America, Europe, and Australia, finding a total value of $202,000,000 for the year 1865; but his estimate of the oriental product far exceeds any English or American opinion upon that subject. For instance, he presents the following table :

Africa	$7,000,000
India	5,500,000
Polynesia	17,000,000
China	31,000,000
Japan	15,000,000
Total	75,500,000

M. Chevalier thus obtains the annexed aggregate for the entire product of the globe after 1848 and before 1865 :

European and American	$202,000,000
Asiatic and African	75,500,000
Total	277,500,000

He supplements this statement by the total quantity which from 1848 to 1864, or during 17 years, was placed at the disposition of the world :

Silver	$1,100,000,000
Gold	3,000,000,000
Total	4,100,000,000

Except for the high estimate of Asiatic production there will be no material dissent from the foregoing conclusions of M. Chevalier. All modern experience indicates that the era of placer mining is soon terminated and must have long since passed away in Asiatic countries. There is little evidence of elaborate methods either of alluvial or mechanical mining, and the sum of $25,000,000 per annum is therefore submitted instead of $75,000,000 as the production of gold and silver beyond the great mining centres.

If we grant the accuracy of M. Chevalier's estimate of the total amount of gold and silver in 1848, and assume that the sum of $250,000,000 per annum will be the average annual production from 1848 to 1880, it will then require the period between those dates, or 30 years, to duplicate the world's supply of precious metals.

The activities of commerce and the developments of human industry, accelerated beyond all former precedent by the progress of the arts, will probably prove sufficient for the absorption of this vast quantity of the precious metals without convulsion of prices or values. The cotton trade with India transferred within seven years $500,000,000 almost entirely in silver. The extension of railways and the construction of works of irrigation in India have absorbed another $500,000,000 of English capital, and there are evidences that the accumulations of European and American wealth are henceforth to be diffused under ample international guarantees over all the continents. If so, there will be ample room and demand for any apparent excess of the precious metals. Europe and America will substitute gold for silver as money, while Asia will probably continue to absorb silver for many years to come, before the ratio of currency to population now existing in Europe shall extend over the eastern world.

A brief statement will illustrate the extent of the oriental demand for the precious metals, which, now mostly confined to silver, will hereafter, or as soon as the world shall desire it, extend to gold. India, in 1857, had a circulating medium of $400,000,000 for the use of a population of 180,000,000, or $2.22 per capita. France has a population of 38,000,000, with a money supply of $910,000,000, or $24 per capita. Suppose China, Japan, and the other industrious populations of Asia to be in the situation of India, and that the current of bullion since 1853 has supplied the Asiatics with $3 per capita, there yet remains a difference of $21 per capita before the monetary level of France is attained, demanding a further supply of $21 per capita over a population of 600,000,000, or not less than $12,600,000,000.

The railway system will soon connect Europe and Asia, and constitutes a most important agency for the transfer of capital and distribution of money among the populations of the eastern continent. Since the suppression of the Indian mutiny an English writer estimates that more than £100,000,000 sterling have been added to the currency and reproductive capacity of India, mostly from England, in the construction of railroads and canals. There were 3,186 miles of railway in operation in 1865, having cost $86,000 per mile, and having been constructed with the aid of a guarantee of five per cent. to stockholders by the province of India. The system for which the government indorsement is already given will be 4,917 miles of railway, at an estimated cost of £77,500,000. These roads will relieve the government of liability when their earnings reach £25 per mile per week, a point which the leading lines have nearly reached, and which all are destined to attain. Such is the success of Indian railways that their connection with Europe by the valley of the Euphrates, and their extension into China, will probably be accomplished within the next 10 years. By that time Russia will have undertaken a railway from Moscow to Pekin through southern Siberia—a great trunk line that would soon justify a series of southern lines penetrating central Asia over those leading caravan routes which have been the avenues of Asiatic commerce for centuries.

If an investment of $430,000,000 in 5,000 miles of railway is financially successful in Hindostan at this time, it may be anticipated that a population of 180,000,000 will warrant the enlargement of the system within the present century fully four-fold, which would be only a fifth of similar communications required and supported by an European or American community. Suppose such a ratio of railway construction extended over China, central and western Asia, and Siberia, it would be only one mile for every 9,000 people, while in the United States there are 36,000 miles for 36,000,000 people, or a mile to every thousand; and yet the Asiatic ratio, moderate as it is, presents the startling result of 66,000 miles of railroad constructed by the expenditure of $5,676,000,000. Such a disbursement of European accumulations in Asia would go far to diffuse not only the blessings of civilization, but any excess of production from the gold and silver mines of the world.

In Australia a railway has been constructed from Melbourne to the Ballarat gold fields, 380 miles, at a cost of $175,000 per mile, which pays a net profit nearly equal to the interest on the immense investment. It is difficult to estimate the amounts destined to be absorbed for railways in all the continents, under the direction of the great powers of the world—projected, constructed, and administered by the wealth and intelligence of America, Russia, England, Germany and France.

GENERAL OBSERVATIONS.

It is deemed expedient to reserve for a subsequent report the detailed statements of mining enterprises east of the Rocky mountains. Many of the organizations for quartz mining in Colorado and Montana yet await the results of scientific investigations into the best methods of reducing the ores of gold and silver; while in the Alleghany district other causes have intervened to postpone a large number of mining operations. The summer of 1868 will doubtless supply the materials of a full and comprehensive report upon this topic.

The act of July 26, 1866, extending facilities for acquiring titles to mineral lands, marks a most important epoch in the progress of mining enterprise upon this continent. Secretary McCulloch, in his report of 1865, suggested that the principle of pre-emption, so long applied to the sale of agricultural lands in the west, should be extended in favor of the holders of claims to gold and silver mines on the public domain. A bill to this effect was furnished to Senator Sherman, which, after much discussion, was matured into the act of July 26, 1866. Under the careful instructions of the Commissioner of the General Land Office, this legislation has been received with great favor on the Pacific slope. By its provisions freedom of exploration, free occupation of government lands for placer mining, a right to pre-empt quartz lodes previously held and improved according to local customs or codes of mining, the right of way for aqueducts or canals, not less essential to agriculture than to mining, and the extension of the homestead and other beneficent provisions of the public land system in favor of settlers upon agricultural lands in mineral districts, have been established as most important elements for the attraction of population and the encouragement of mining enterprises. The Commissioner of the Land Office has carefully analyzed this enactment, and greatly facilitated its execution by a circular recently issued. The spirit of the legislation under consideration is in the interest of actual settlement and occupation, and adverse to absentee ownership for merely speculative purposes of mining properties. It will probably be necessary to supplement the act in question by some general revision of the local mining customs, which, although generally founded on the Spanish code so long in use in Mexico, are often incongruous and obscure.

The most practicable, and economical methods of desulphurizing the refractory ores which characterize the Atlantic mines having been made by the Secretary a special subject of inquiry, no effort will be made on the present occasion to anticipate its progress and conclusions.

I beg leave to renew a former suggestion, that the metalliferous localities of the Alleghanies south of the Potomac river shall be carefully explored under national auspices.

JAMES W. TAYLOR.

Hon. Hugh McCulloch,
    Secretary of the Treasury

APPENDIX.

SECTION I.

ARTESIAN WELLS

[Extract from a geological reconnoissance of Arkansas, by David Dale Owen, in 1859'-'60.]

It may be useful and interesting in this place to say a few words in regard to a few indi-·idual artesian wells of particular interest, either on account of their great depth, their large diameter, or the great volume of water which they afford.

One of the most interesting artesian wells bored in the valley of the Ohio is that sunk by Messrs. C. J. and A. B. Dupont, in the city of Louisville, This well is three inches in the bore, and 2,086 feet deep. The water flows from this well at the rate of 330,000 gallons in 24 hours, or 264 gallons per minute, with a mechanical force equal to a 10-horse power steam engine. The water rises by its own pressure, when confined in tubes, 170 feet above the surface. When the whole force of the water is allowed to expend itself on the central jet, it is projected 100 feet, settling down to a steady flow of a stream 60 feet high at the above rate of 330,000 gallons in the 24 hours. The water is perfectly clear of a temperature of 76½° Fahrenheit, the year round. It is highly charged with mineral properties, being a strong saline, sulphuretted water, similar in its composition and medical properties to the celebrated Kissinger waters of Bavaria, and the Blue Licks of Kentucky. This well was commenced in April, 1857, and completed in 16 months.

The well bored by Mr. William H. Belcher, of St. Louis, was commenced in 1849, and in 1853 was 1,590 feet deep, at which depth a copious stream of "sulphur water issues," which is said to be similar in its properties to the Blue Lick water of Kentucky.

This well was commenced as a cistern, at the surface of the ground, 14 feet diameter; at 30 feet deep, 6 feet diameter; thence it diminishes to 16 inches diameter, at 78 feet deep. The bore is then 9 inches, and this diameter is continued to 457 feet; thence to the depth of 1,509 feet it is 3½ inches.

At 550 feet, at the top of a limestone, the water became salty; 200 feet below this, in a layer of shale, the water contained 1⅞ per cent. of salt. At 965 feet, below a bed of bitumin-ous marl, the water contained 2¼ per cent. of salt. The hardest rock was a bed of chert, at a depth of ·1,179 feet, and 62 feet thick. In this rock the water contained 3 per cent. of salt.

This well was commenced in the spring of 1849, and reached its depth of 2,199 feet on the 12th of March, 1854. During these five years the work was at times intermitted for months, so that the time actually employed was only 33 months, and cost about $10,000. There is a constant flow of water from this well of 75 gallons per minute.

Three artesian wells have been bored at Columbus, Ohio. The first was carried 110 feet; but not reaching the rock, was abandoned, the quicksand coming in in such quantities that they could not exclude it by tubing.

The second well was tubed down 54 feet, with cast-iron piping, six inches interior diameter. The boring was then continued to the rock, 122 feet. Wrought-iron pipes of smaller size were forced down, but broke at the second joint from the lower end. The pipe was with-drawn, and a pump let down, when the well was found to be cleared of obstructions to the rock. The reamer was then sent down, and went freely till at the depth of 100 feet it began to rub. The pump was then sent down; the well had become filled with sand and gravel 66 feet, and after prolonged labor, it was ascertained that the sand ran into the well as fast as it could be taken out. Various contrivances were resorted to to stop this obstruction, but without effect; so that, on the 4th of November, 1857, this boring was also abandoned. A contract was now made on the 4th of November with Mr. Fleming Spangler to bore a new well, with the understanding that he was to tube it into the rock within 18 or 20 days,, or receive no pay.

The new well was commenced by sinking a pit, and cribbing it down with circular crib-bing, which, on the 16th day of November, reached the depth of 29 feet. After considerable labor, by alternate boring and tubing, Mr. Spangler finally succeeded on the 31st of January, 1858, in penetrating the limestone rock 248 feet, at a depth of 371 feet from the surface. He then contracted to bore to the depth of 1,000 feet from the surface for $1 50 per foot. having thus far averaged about five to six feet in the rock-borings per day.

A vein of sulphur water was struck at 180 feet on the 22d of December, 1857. The borings were continued, with occasional cessation of labor, up to the 11th of December, having then reached a depth of 1,858 feet, without, however, up to that date having reached any consid-erable body of artesian water, and it is probable from the details of the borings that they will have to go from 300 to 500 feet more through blue limestones, marly shales, and Ken-tucky river marble-rock, before reaching the porous sandstones, in which there is the best chance of obtaining a body of water.

In the valley of the Ohio, the two great reservoirs of artesian water are the two great porous sandstones, alternating with and resting on the shales, which form the impervious layers that hold up the water. One of these great sandstone series constitutes the mill-stone grit at the base of the coal measures; the other, the lowest fossiliferous sandstones and calciferous sand-rock, subordinate to the blue limestone and Kentucky river marble-rock of the west.

The water obtained in the first of these reservoirs is almost invariably a strong brine; in the latter, so far as experience goes it is a mineral water, strongly charged with a variety of saline substances, and impregnated with sulphuretted hydrogen gas; hence, though the two first artesian borings, cited above, were eminently successful, as far as obtaining a large body of mineral water was concerned, yet they may be considered entire failures, as far as obtaining a body of pure water fit for manufacturing purposes, or domestic use.

Both these water horizons exist in Arkansas; in fact, the millstone grit, as already stated, has a most extraordinary development in that State, and many localities have been, and will hereafter be recorded, where profitable brines might be obtained in this geological formation, by a judicious selection of locality, and well conducted, systematic borings.

There are also other water horizons in the southern counties of Arkansas, which can be reached by borings through the tertiary and cretaceous formations; but, so far as experience goes, artesian waters obtained therefrom will be more or less charged with mineral matter.

As we have some of the records of an artesian well sunk through equivalent formations at Charleston, South Carolina, it may be well in this place to give a few of the statistics of this boring.

Few wells have presented as many difficuties, or called for greater skill and perseverance in the engineer. The surface soil is loose sand for 20 feet, the lower half of which is saturated with water; next a stiff, compact clay, about 40 feet thick, also water-bearing. At 60 feet, firm marl commences, alternating with some rock more or less indurated, in all 150 feet thick. Below this occur the cretaceous strata, differing but little lithologically from the layers of the tertiary formation above; both formations being alternations of firm marl, sandstone, and loose sands, alternating with layers of hard limestone, seldom containing less than 20 per cent. of carbonate of lime. Fifty-four rocks, varying from 2 to 10 feet each, and measuring in the aggregate 250 feet, were penetrated by the boring. Cast-iron tubes, six feet interior diameter, were sunk 80 feet to exclude superficial sands: but these gradually worked their way down, and continued to flow under the bottom of the tube. Finally, however, the solid rock was reached at 230 feet. But even here the difficulties did not end; for, under each solid rock, quick or loose sand generally occurred, and flowed into the well, so as often to fill it up, and sometimes almost instantly, 60 to 100 feet. Large chambers were thus formed under many of the rock strata. Sometimes, in the morning, the well would be found filled 50 to 100 feet, and even 140 feet, with sand. At 700 feet, so much sand continued to flow in as to render it impossible to proceed, and there was no resource but to tube down into it and through it, and to do this the well had to be reamed out to a larger size, thus taxing the ingenuity of the engineer severely to overcome all the various obstacles to success. At 1,020 feet the sands again came in, so as frequently to fill up the well 100 feet; but the difficulty was finally overcome by retubing with larger wrought-iron tubes, which were sunk to 1,102 feet, and the boring continued 43 feet lower, or 1,145 feet. The temperature at 900 feet was 82¼° Fahrenheit.

Subsequent to this date, the Charleston well was sunk to the depth of 1,250 feet, and yields 30,000 gallons of water in 24 hours, which rises 10 feet above the surface. Another has now been commenced at the same place, 12 inches in diameter, and has already reached the depth of 1,000 feet.

On the 22d of April, 1857, an artesian well was commenced at Lafayette, Indiana, and, after sinking to the depth of 216 feet, a vein of water finally overflowed the well on the 18th of February, 1858. The boring was then continued to the depth of 230 feet. Great delay and an unnecessary cost of $1,000 were incurred, in consequence of one of the cast-iron pipes breaking in being forced into its place. This well delivered on the 3d of September one wine gallon of mineral water in 15.8 seconds, which is equal to a discharge of 1,468 gallons in 24 hours, sufficient, if the surplus water be properly saved, for all the purposes of a first-class watering place. This mineral water contains, according to Dr. C. M. Wetherill, 400 grains of solid matter to the gallon. For an analysis of this water, I refer the reader to the report on this well, made by C. M. Wetherill, Ph. D., M. D.

The well from which the name Artesian was originally derived was bored more than a century ago at Aire, in Artois, in France, and has flowed steadily ever since. The water rises 11 feet above the ground, and supplies nearly 250 gallons per minute.

The Grenelle well, at Paris, was commenced in 1834 and completed in 1841, at which time the rod suddenly descended several feet, and shortly after the water rose to the surface in vast quantities. For the first 50 feet the boring was 12 inches in diameter, which was reduced to nine inches, and then carried to a depth of 1,100 feet; a further reduction was made to seven and a half inches, until the depth of 1,300 feet was reached; and a final diminution to six inches, till the termination of the well at 1,806 feet. From the completion of the well to the present time there has been a steady flow of over 500,000 gallons in 24 hours, of a temperature of 81° Fahrenheit.

3 T

The Kissinger well in Bavaria is 1,878 feet; the last 139 feet the boring passes through rock salt. From this well 100 cubic feet of water gushes forth every minute. The water contains 3½ per cent. of salt.

The artesian well at the Bois de Boulogne is over 39 inches in diameter. This well was bored by a peculiar drill, weighing about 3,500 pounds, managed by a grapple, which opens as it descends, and then closes, when it is raised by means of a parallelogram connected at the angles with two cords reaching up to the top of the well, where they may be managed with the hand, or by means of machinery. The drill below is constructed with seven teeth of cast steel, fitted to drive into the bed of rock, or abrade it. The drill has a shank by which it may be seized and lifted. The whole is worked by a 24 to 30 horse-power engine. The grapple closes at the bottom, seizing the handle of the drill, then rises with the drill several feet, opens, and lets the drill fall. Thus the drill rises and falls 20 or 30 times a minute. After working 12 hours, the rods are taken out, the sand pump let down, and the sand and mud withdrawn, and the rods, grapple, and drill again let down and set to work. To work this apparatus requires only six men, and the cost of working is about $3 per foot.

In 1857, this well had reached a depth of 1,427 feet, and they hoped in October to reach the main source of water below the chalk.

In the month of May, 1858, the French engineer, M. Jus, commenced boring an artesian well in the Sahara desert, Africa, in the province of Constantine; and on the 19th of June a jet of water of about 1,000 gallons per minute flowed from the bowels of the earth, at a temperature of 61°. 24 Fahrenheit. The joy of the inhabitants was unbounded when they witnessed this extraordinary spectacle, and caused them to regard a people who could bring about such a marvel as to cause water to gush forth from the arid desert as truly beings of a superior race.

Subsequently four other wells were bored in the desert: one at Temakin, yielding eight gallons per minute; one in the oasis of Tamelhat, which gave 120 litres of water per minute; one in the oasis of Sidi Nached, yielding 4,300 litres of water from the depth of 54 metres, the oasis having been completely ruined by drought; one also in Oum Thior, which yields 108 litres of water per minute; and a sixth well has been sunk at Shegga.

A remarkable artesian well was bored at Bourne, in England. The borings passed through two strata of limestone, with other intervening strata, to the depth of only 92 feet. The bore is only four inches, and this supplies the town through mains and smaller pipes and plugs for fires, the pressure being sufficient to throw water over the buildings. It delivers 557,000 gallons per day. It rises at the town hall 39 feet 9 inches.

These are a few of the statistics of some of the most interesting artesian wells both in this country and in Europe; they give some details of the cost, mode of boring, and difficulties to be encountered, that will be interesting and useful to the readers of this report.

The conditions necessary to the successful boring of an artesian well are:

First. A fountain head more elevated than the locality where the boring is to be undertaken.

Second. A gentle inclination or moderate dip from the fountain head towards the locality of the well.

Third. Alternations of porous and impervious strata, beneath the drainage of the country.

The fountain head need not be in the immediate vicinity; on the contrary, it is often far distant—40 to 100 miles or more. If it forms the elevated rim of a large basin, from which the strata dip in all directions towards its centre, it. is all the more favorable for artesian borings within that basin. If the geological formations form a synclinal fold or trough, the fountain head being on the anticlinals of the ridges more or less parallel, this is also a favorable position for artesian borings.

The flow of water from the fountain head, held up by the impervious strata beneath, and permeating the porous superincumbent layers, may be arrested, however, even without such a structure of the country, by being dammed up by local barriers, which may either be impervious fissures, cutting the strata more or less at right angles, or extensive faults filled up with clay, which is a very common occurrence.

A steep or high angle of inclination of dip is always an unfavorable structure of country, because in such situations the water flows away beyond the reach of artesian borings, which must necessarily cut the strata at such an acute angle as to pass through only a few layers of rock. Without a knowledge of the internal structure of the geological formations which lie deep-seated, very little clue can be obtained to the selection of a favorable locality by a simple inspection of the physical condition of the surface of the country. For instance, a perfectly level plain, with no hills in sight, may be more favorable for artesian wells than an undulating country, simply from the fact of its having a higher fountain head.

The third condition mentioned above, namely, alternation of porous and impervious strata, is almost everywhere to be met with.

SECTION II.

LIGNITES OF THE WEST.

[Abstract from report of F. V. Hayden, United States geologist for Nebraska, to Commissioner of General Land Office, from Silliman's Journal of March, 1868.]

The construction of the Pacific railroads across the continent is bringing about the dawn of a new era in the progress of the west. Already has the Union Pacific railroad, from Omaha, struck the first range of the Rocky mountains, more than 525 miles west of the Missouri river. The earth is now called upon more earnestly than ever before to yield up her treasures of gold, silver, copper, iron, and mineral fuel, and the existence of the last two minerals in the west, in workable quantities, is one of the most important practical questions of the day. It is my purpose in this article merely to state briefly some observations made last autumn in regard to the lignite deposits of Colorado and Dakota Territories. The details will be given more fully in the final report of the geological survey of Nebraska, now in progress of preparation.

The discovery that large deposits of "stone coal," as it is often called by travellers, existed in various portions of the west is by no means a new one at the present time. The lignite beds of the upper Missouri were noticed by Lewis and Clark, 1803 and 1804, those of Laramie plains by Fremont, 1842, and those of the Raton mountain region by General Emory as far back as 1848. But the intense interest with which they are regarded now, as a source of fuel to the vast stretch of fertile but almost treeless plains, has been created anew by the advancing westward wave brought about by the construction of those great national highways. The fact, also, that the coal deposits of Iowa and Missouri are restricted in area, and the coal limited in quantity, and in most cases inferior in quality, and that west of these States it may be said that there is no true coal at all, renders any source of fuel in the far west a matter of the greatest importance. In the valley of the Missouri river and the Yellowstone there are numerous beds of tertiary lignite, varying from a few inches to seven feet in thickness. These formations have been described many times, and until the Northern Pacific railroad is carried through that region they will remain of little practical importance. But the Union Pacific railroad is now in progress of construction through the lignite deposits of the Laramie plains, and the Union Pacific railway, eastern division, and the branch from Denver to Cheyenne City, will pass through those of Colorado, so that if the lignite beds and iron mines of this region are of such a character as to be of economical use, the time for their demand has already come.

My examination of the geology of the State of Nebraska, during the past season, failed to develop any workable beds of coal within the limits of that State. My attention was then directed to the great lignite deposits of the Laramie plains. I found the lignite of excellent quality in beds from 5 to 11 feet thick, and I estimated the area occupied by this basin at 5,000 square miles. Its most eastern limit is about 10 miles east of Rock creek, a branch of the Medicine Bow river. Outcroppings have been seen all along Rock creek, Medicine Bow, on Rattlesnake Hills, on the North Platte, Muddy creek, all along Bitter creek, Ham's Fork, Echo Cañon, and all along Weber river, nearly to Great Salt lake, showing that one connected series of deposits covers this whole area. The lignite taken from the beds on Rock creek is from the outcroppings, yet it burns with a bright red flame, giving out a good degree of heat, leaving scarcely any ash, and is quite as desirable fuel for domestic purposes as any wood. It is non-bituminous, exhibits just a trace of sulphuret of iron, which, decomposing, gives a rusty reddish appearance to the outcrops, and there are seams of jet, 1 to 12 inches in thickness, which looks much like cannel coal, and is thus termed by the miners. The Union Pacific railroad will pass directly through these great coal fields, and as most of the freight will go westward for many years, the cars on their return can be loaded with this lignite, thus to be distributed through Nebraska at a cost much less than that of wood at the present time. There are also indications of an abundance of iron ore in the vicinity of these deposits, and the Union Pacific Railroad Company contemplate establishing rolling mills in the Laramie plains at no distant period.

The next point visited was South Boulder creek, the Marshall mines, which are probably the most valuable in the west. I made a pretty careful examination of these mines, as they have been wrought for four or five years. An average of 50 tons is taken from this place daily and sold at Denver, at prices varying from $12 to $15 per ton. The beds are at the foot of the mountains, and dip to such an extent as to expose the whole series, 11 in number, varying from 5 to 13 feet in thickness, so that we have from 30 to 50 feet at least of solid lignite. This is the most favorable locality for studying the strata enclosing the lignite that I have ever met with in the west, and this is due to several causes, the principal of which is their proximity to the base of the mountains, by which they are elevated at a moderate angle. The following somewhat remarkable section is approximately correct, at least:

45. Sandstone, gray and rather coarse grained.
44. Drab clay.
43. Lignite.
42. Drab clay.
41. Lignite.
40. Drab clay.
39. Sandstone.
38. Drab clay.
37. Lignite.
36. Drab clay.
35. Sandstone.
34. Drab clay, 10 to 12 feet.
33. Sandstone.
32. Drab clay.
31. Lignite.
30. Drab clay.
29. Sandstone.
28. Drab clay passing up into sand three feet.
27. Lignite, 5 feet.
26. Drab clay, 5 feet.
25. Sandstone, 14 feet.
24. Drab clay, 3 feet.
23. Lignite, 7½ feet.

22. Drab clay, 5 feet.
21. Sandstone, 20 feet.
20. Drab clay, 3 feet.
19. Lignite, 7 feet.
18. Drab clay, 3 feet.
17. Sandstone, 40 feet.
16. Drab clay, 3 feet.
15. Lignite, 5 feet.
14. Drab clay.
13. Sandstone.
12. Drab clay.
11. Lignite.
10. Drab clay.
9. Sandstone.
8. Drab clay.
7. Lignite, 5 feet.
6. Drab clay.
5. Gray and yellowish gray sandstone.
4. Drab clay, 3 feet.
3. Lignite, 11 to 13 feet.
2. Drab clay, 4 feet.
1. Fine yellowish grit indurated cretaceous beds, 1, 2, 3, 4, &c.

The thickness of the beds is given when it could be obtained with any degree of accuracy. It is barely possible that beds 6 to 13 feet inclusive have been broken down from the summit of the upheaval just beyond and thus displaced. The inclination of the strata from 1 to 16 inclusive is 8° east, and the cleavage of the beds of lignite is vertical and exactly parallel with the dip. From 13 to 29, inclination is 40°, and the remainder 35°. Lignite beds 38 and 42 have not yet been tested, and very little is known of them. They have been exposed in the search for iron ore. The summit of the hills above all these beds in the section is covered with a large thickness of superficial drift material, which undoubtedly conceals many other beds which properly belong to the section. Mines have been opened on Coal creek, three miles south of Marshall's mines, but they have been abandoned for the present. Another has been opened about 20 miles south of Cheyenne City, on Pole creek. The drift began with an outcropping of about four feet eight inches in thickness, inclination 12° east. The lignite grows better in quality as it is wrought further into the earth, and the bed, by following the dip 200 feet, is found to be five feet four inches thick, and the lignite is sold readily at Cheyenne City for $25 per ton. The beds are so concealed by a superficial drift deposit that it is difficult to obtain a clearly connected section of the rocks. A section across the inclined edges of the beds eastward from the mountains is as follows:

7. Drab clay passing up into areno-calcareous grit composed of an aggregation of oyster shells, *ostreasubtrigonalis*.
6. Lignite, 5 to 6 feet.
5. Drab clay, 4 to 6 feet.
4. Reddish rusty sandstone in thin laminæ, 20 feet.
3. Drab arenaceous clay, indurated.
2. Massive sandstone, 50 feet.
1. No. 5 cretaceous, apparently passing up into a yellowish sandstone.

The summit of the hills near this bed of lignite is covered with loose oyster shells, and there must have been a thickness of four feet or more almost entirely composed of them. The species seems to be identical with the one found in a similar geological position in the lower lignite beds of the upper Missouri, near Fort Clark, and at the mouth of the Judith river, and doubtless was an inhabitant of the brackish waters which must have existed about the dawn of the tertiary period in the west. No other shells were found in connection with these in Colorado, but on the upper Missouri well-known fresh-water types exist in close proximity, showing that if it proves anything it rather affirms the eocene age of these lower lignite beds. These lignite beds are exposed in many localities all along the eastern base of the mountains, and from the best information I can secure I have estimated the area occupied by them north of the Arkansas river at 5,000 square miles. According to the explorations of Dr. John L. Le Conte during the past season, which are of great interest, these same lignite formations extend far southward into New Mexico, on both sides of the Rocky mountains. Specimens of lignite brought from the Raton mountains by Dr. Le Conte resemble very closely in appearance and color the anthracites of Pennsylvania. It is probable that no true coal will ever be found west of longitude 96°, and it becomes, therefore, a most important question to ascertain the real value of these vast deposits of lignite for fuel and other economical purposes. Can these lignites be employed for generating steam and smelting ores? In regard to the lignites in the Laramie plains I have as yet seen no analysis, but specimens are now in the hands of Dr. Torrey, of New York, for that purpose. Specimens from Marshall's mine on South Boulder creek were submitted to Dr. Torrey by the Union Pacific Railroad Company for examination, with the following result:

Water in a state of combination, or its elements	12.00
Volatile matter expelled at a red heat, forming inflammable gases and vapors	26.00
Fixed carbon	59.20
Ash of a reddish color, sometimes gray	2.80
	100.00

A specimen from Coal creek, three miles south, yielded similar results:

Water in a state of combination, or probably its elements, as in dry wood	20.00
Volatile matter expelled at a red heat, in the form of inflammable gases and vapors	19.30
Fixed carbon	58.70
Ash, consisting chiefly of oxyd of iron, alumina, and a little silica	2.00
	100.00

The percentage of carbon is shown to be in one case 59.20, and in the other 58.70, which shows at a glance the superiority of the western lignites over those found in any other portion of the world. Anthracite is regarded as so much superior a fuel on account of the large per cent. of carbon, and also the small amount of hydrogen and oxygen. The bituminous coals contain a large percentage of hydrogen and oxygen, but not enough water and ash to prevent them from being made useful, but the calorific power of lignite is very much diminished by the quantity of water contained in it, from the fact that so valuable a portion of the fuel must be used in converting that water into steam.

The day of my visit to the Marshall coal mines, on South Boulder creek, 73 tons of lignite were taken out and sold at the rate of $4 a ton at the mine, and from $12 to $16 at Denver. This lignite is somewhat brittle, but has nearly the hardness of ordinary anthracite, which it very much resembles at a distance.

In some portions there is a considerable quantity of amber. I spent two evenings at Mr. Marshall's house burning this fuel in a furnace, and it seemed to me that it would prove to be superior to ordinary western bituminous coals and rank next to anthracite for domestic purposes. Being non-bituminous, it will require a draught to burn well. It is as neat as anthracite, leaving no stain on the fingers. It produces no offensive gas or odor, and is thus superior in a sanitary point of view, and when brought into general use it will be a great favorite for culinary purposes. It contains no destructive elements, leaves very little ash, no clinkers, and produces no more erosive effects on stoves, grates, or steam boilers than dry wood. If exposed in the open air it is apt to crumble, but if protected it receives no special injury. Dr. Torrey thinks there is no reason why it should not be eminently useful for generating steam and for smelting ores.

Throughout the intercalated beds of clay at Boulder creek and vicinity are found masses of a kind of concretionary iron ore, varying in size from one ounce to several tons in weight. This iron ore is probably a *limonite*, commonly known under the name of brown hematite or brown iron ore. It may perhaps be found in the state of carbonate of iron when sought for beyond the reach of the atmosphere. These nodules or concretionary masses, when broken, show regular concentric rings, varying in color from yellow to brown, looking sometimes like rusty yellow agates. It is said to yield 70 per cent. of metallic iron. The first smelting furnace ever created in Colorado was established here by Mr. Marshall, and he informed me that for the production of one ton of pig iron three tons of the ore, 200 pounds of limestone, and 130 to 150 bushels of charcoal are required. Over 500 tons of this ore have been taken from this locality, and the area over which it seems to abound cannot be less than 50 square miles. Indications of large deposits of iron ore have been found in many other localities along the line of the Pacific railroads, and if the mineral fuel which is found here in such great abundance can be made useful for smelting purposes, these lignites and iron ore beds will exert the same kind of influence over the progress of the great west that Pennsylvania exerts over all the contiguous States. When we reflect that we have from 10,000 to 20,000 square miles of mineral fuel in the centre of a region where for a radius of 600 to 1,000 miles in every direction there is little or no fuel either on or beneath the surface, the future value of these deposits cannot be overestimated.

The geological age of these western lignite deposits is undoubtedly tertiary. Those on the upper Missouri have been shown to be of that age, both from vegetable and animal remains, and in the Laramie plains I collected two species of plants, a *populus* and a *plantanus*, specifically identical with those found on the upper Missouri. The simple fact that cretaceous formations Nos. 1, 2, 3, 4, and 5 are well shown all along the foot of the mountains, and that No. 5 presents its usual lithological character, with its peculiar fossils, within 15 miles of Marshall's mines; also that at the mine 2, 3, and 4 are seen inclining at nearly the same angle and holding a lower position than the lignite beds, is sufficient evidence that the strata enclosing the lignite beds are newer than cretaceous. A few obscure dicotyledonous leaves were found, which belong rather to tertiary forms than cretaceous.

The connection of the lignite deposits on the upper Missouri has been traced uninterruptedly to the North Platte, about 80 miles above Fort Laramie. They then pass beneath the White river tertiary beds, but reappear again about 20 miles south of Pole creek, and continue far southward into New Mexico. Near Red Buttes, on the North Platte, it seems also probable that the same basin continues northward along the slope of the Rocky mountains, nearly or quite to the Arctic sea. Whether or not there are any indications of this formation over the eastern range into the British possessions I have no means of ascertaining, but the Wind River chain, which forms the main divide of the Rocky Mountain range, exhibits a great thickness of the lignite tertiary beds on both eastern and western slopes, showing conclusively by the fracture and inclination of the strata that prior to the elevation of this range they extended uninterruptedly in a horizontal position across the area now occupied by the Wind River chain. Passing the first range of mountains in the Laramie plains we find that the Big Laramie river cuts through cretaceous beds Nos. 2 and 3; continuing our course westward to Little Laramie, a branch of the Big Laramie, and No. 3 becomes 50 to 150 feet in thickness, filled with fossils, *Ostrea congesta*, and a species of *Inoceramus*. At Rock creek, about 40 miles west of Big Laramie river, the lignite beds overlap the cretaceous, but in such a way as to show that the more inclined portions have been swept away by erosion, and that the red beds and carboniferous limestones once existed without break and in a horizontal position across the Laramie range prior to its elevation.

I cannot discuss this matter in detail in this article, but the evidence is clear to me now that all the lignite tertiary beds of the west are but fragments of one great basin, interrupted here and there by the upheaval of mountain chains or concealed by the deposition of newer formations. All the evidence that I can secure seems to indicate that there are no valuable beds of lignite west of the Mississippi in formations older than the tertiary.

SECTION III.

MINERAL RESOURCES OF THE TERRITORY OF MONTANA.

[By W. S. Keyes, M. E.]

The Territory of Montana is, saving the recently acquired Alaska, the newest and most remote of the subdivisions of the domain of the United States. Its form is very nearly exactly a right-angled parallelogram, the irregularity of the figure occurring on the southwestern border, where the territorial limits are coincident with the main chain of the Cœur d'Alene and Bitter Root mountains. Its northern boundary is latitude 49°, being the dividing line between the British and American possessions. Its longitudinal extension, with Dakota on the east and Idaho on the west, embraces 12 degrees, viz: from 27° to 39° west of the meridian of Washington, while its southern boundary is marked, excepting a small portion on the extreme southwest, by the 45th parallel of north latitude.

HISTORICAL.—Our first authentic description of that portion of the continent, of which Montana now forms a part, is due to the labors of Captains Lewis and Clarke, two officers of the regular United States army. They were despatched, at the beginning of the present century, under the auspices of the general government, to explore the far northwest, which was then, and has remained until quite recently, almost a *terra incognita*. With infinite patience they surmounted all the natural obstacles in their pathway; climbed the snowy ranges; sought out the passes in the mountains; descended in canoes all the principal streams, and pursued to their sources by far the greater number of their tributaries; passed some years among the Indians; gave names to all the rivers, by far the larger proportion of which are still retained; described the fauna and flora—in a word, all the animal and vegetable life, so exhaustively that their descriptions, perfectly accurate more than 60 years ago, are in every essential particular as truthful to-day.

Again, we have the results of the labors of Captain Bonneville, who explored these regions some 30 years subsequently to Lewis and Clarke. The graphic pen of the late Washington Irving compiled from these observations a most admirable and interesting volume.

More recently we have the report of Governor Isaac I. Stevens, who, in the years 1853, 1854, and 1855, made a careful survey of the passes of the Rocky mountains, with a view to determine the practicability of a northern route for a railroad to the Pacific. Lieutenant Mullan, one of the members of the party, established a wagon route from Fort Benton, on the Missouri river, to Walla-Walla, on the Columbia river, in Washington Territory. The distance between these points does not exceed 650 miles, and with this, comparatively speaking, trifling land portage we unite by navigable streams the waters of the Pacific ocean and those of the Gulf of Mexico.

Up to May 26, 1864, on which date the organic act creating the Territory was approved by Congress, Montana was embraced within the jurisdiction of Idaho, whose laws still remained in force until the assembling of the first territorial legislature at Bannock, December 12, of the same year. During the interregnum no advantage was taken or sought to be taken of the technical irregularity of administering in Montana the laws of Idaho—a fact which bears eloquent testimony to the integrity and high character of the first settlers. Subsequently, when the fame of its rich placers had been noised abroad, the Territory became flooded with an immigration of ruffians, notorious desperadoes, and cutthroats, the refuse of the Pacific States and Territories. Encouraged by impunity, their leaders sought and obtained such positions in the lower executive ranks of the government that justice against any member or members of the band having its ramifications throughout the entire mining regions was practically impossible. The people enduring "until longer endurance ceased to be a virtue," were impelled to the formation of a "vigilance committee."

This organization, which still exists, finally triumphed over the lawless desperadoes who infested the country; hung some and banished others, until life and property in Montana were as safe if not safer than in the more settled portions of the United States. The civil law and its expositors are now able, unaided, to fulfil to the utmost the behests of justice and to stifle at once, if not entirely prevent, any recurrence of such outrages as led to the formation of a committee of vigilance.

The name of the Territory is derived directly from the Spanish, in which language the word "montaña" signifies "mountain," while the aboriginal designation in the Snake dialect, viz: "Toi-abe shock-up," "land of the mountain," likewise bears testimony to the broken character of its surface.

Area.—According to J. L. Corbett, chief engineer, the area of the Territory is 146,689.35 square miles, equal to 93,881,184 acres. Compared with the older and settled portions of the United States, Montana is nearly as large as the State of California, somewhat more than half the size of Texas, nearly three times that of New York, two and one-half times that of the six New England States combined, four times that of Kentucky, and 110 times that of Rhode Island.

The proportion susceptible of cultivation in the several counties is, according to the same authority, as follows:

Counties.	Meadow.	Arable.	Terrace land.
Gallatin	32,000	195,040	64,000
Madison	21,000	39,000	44,000
Deer Lodge	23,000	91,200	28,000
Missoula	52,000	114,000	35,000
Big Horn	96,800	1,592,250	152,800
Beaver Head	18,500	34,500	38,000
Jefferson	31,200	45,400	....
Edgerton	25,320	38,000	....
Chouteau	78,000	372,400	85,000
	377,800	2,521,800	446,800

Being a grand total of 3,346,400 acres, which gives a proportion of little more than 1 in 30. In the absence of the official returns of the surveyor general, these figures must be taken only as reasonable approximations.

Discovery of Gold.—None of the earlier exploring parties seem to have observed or even predicted the probability of finding the precious metals in any of the far northwestern Territories. Professor Dana, it is true, mentions in 1842 the occurrence of certain gold-bearing talcose and micaceous shists on the Umpqua river, in southern Oregon, and likewise stated that similar rocks had been found on the banks of the Sacramento river, in California. Saving the Indians, the inhabitants of these regions consisted of a few trappers and a small number of Catholic missionaries. The latter, from their intelligence and cultivation, were the only persons likely to have noticed the geological significance of the rocks, drift, and alluvium ; but even had they been well aware of the existence of gold and silver—and this, on the authority of Father De Smet, was indeed the case—it is highly improbable that they would have laid much stress on the advantages to accrue from their development.

These self-denying pioneers of civilization have ever shown themselves to be the only body of men who, within the domain of the United States, have been able to tame the savages and introduce among them the arts of peace. Strictly upright in their commerce with the aborigines, they have succeeded in obtaining their confidence, and while the houses of the settlers are set in flames, and themselves and their families fall a prey to the tomahawk, these missionary establishments always remain intact.

To Mr. Granville Stuart, an old resident and careful observer, we are indebted for the following facts in regard to the early history of gold-seeking in what now constitutes Montana.

It seems that one Francois Finlay, commonly known as "Benetsee," a half-breed, from the Red River of the North, in British territory, had for some time worked in the placers of California. Becoming dissatisfied with that country, he found his way back again to the vicinity of his former home. He arrived in Montana, and was the first person to discover on Gold creek a few particles of fine float gold. This creek is situated in Deer Lodge county, on the western slope of the Rocky mountains, and is one of the minor tributaries of the Hell Gate river, whose waters flow ultimately into the Pacific ocean. Probably from a lack of provisions he did little more than superficially prospect the locality. He performed, however, enough work to entitle him to the honor of discovery.

Subsequently, in May, 1858, James and Granville Stuart, Thomas Adams, and Reese Anderson prospected on Gold creek, finding as high as ten cents to the pan, equalling about one-half cent to the pound of earth. This party, few in numbers and continually annoyed by the Blackfeet Indians, who persistently stole their horses, and being, moreover, unsupplied with the necessary tools and provisions, likewise abandoned, for the moment, any further search.

Two years later, namely, during the summer of 1860, one Henry Thomas, called "Gold Tom," or "Tom Gold Digger," set up on Gold creek three small sluice-boxes which he had himself roughly hewed out of green timber. With these rude implements he succeeded, unaided and alone, in collecting from $1 50 to $2 per day. His was the first actual mining in that part of Washington Territory now Montana. Becoming dissatisfied with the reward of his labors, he kept industriously prospecting all over the Territory, and, strangely enough, his favorite camping ground was near the location of the present city of Helena, in whose immediate vicinity were found, subsequently, some of the richest placer deposits ever worked.

It remained, however, for others than "Gold Tom" to unearth the precious dust whose resting place had been so often pressed by his footstep. Stuart and his party had removed to the vicinity of Fort Bridger, on the emigrant road, where they lived as traders, until, in 1860, they concluded to return and thoroughly investigate the affluents to the valley of the Deer Lodge. They prospected during 1861, and found several favorable localities. It was not, however, until 1862, and after they had received from Walla-Walla, 425 miles distant, both tools and lumber, that the first string of ten real sluices was set up and worked. In the mean time they had communicated the news of their discovery to a relative at Pike's Peak, as Colorado was then called. Hence resulted a considerable exodus of miners, who began to arrive in Deer Lodge about June 20, 1862. The new comers discovered the placers at Pike's Peak gulch, Pioneer gulch, &c. From this time forward the immigration of gold seekers rapidly increased in volume. Many, becoming bewildered among the pathless hills while searching for the Deer Lodge, discovered other and valuable placers. At present there remains scarcely a mountain gorge or sequestered ravine but has been prospected more or less thoroughly from mouth to source.

For several months anterior to the segregation of the Territory from Idaho the people governed themselves. Far away from any settled habitations, a little handful of hardy mining adventurers, they still found time, amid the excitements of gold-mining, to take such steps as have finally secured the fullest liberty combined with an entire subservience to law. They discovered the placers at Bannock, began the development of Alder gulch, and laid the foundation of Virginia City, now the capital of Montana, months before the arrival of any territorial officials.

POPULATION.—The present population of the Territory may be estimated to be about 24,000 souls. This total has been arrived at from the reports of the different assistant assessors of internal revenue, who have received instructions to make an informal approximate census. Mr. N. P. Langford, the efficient United States collector and one of the pioneers of Montana, is of the opinion that the number of inhabitants has remained very nearly constant from the fall of 1864 up to and including the present year, and has probably, during that interval, never fallen below 21,000.

We may, by still another method, obtain a reasonable approximation, corroborative of the foregoing, viz., by an examination of the vote cast in September of the present year. Local causes combined with political excitement, caused the casting of an unexpectedly large and probably full vote. The eight counties into which the Territory was originally divided, not including Big Horn, polled a total of very nearly 12,000 votes. In this number are included the votes of the soldiers performing volunteer service against the Indians, all the colored votes, and also those which were rejected from the count by reason of informality. Hence, multiplying the full vote by two, we have a total population of 24,000, corresponding with that reported by the assistant assessors. In support of this multiple, which may by some be deemed unreasonably small, it may be alleged that the Territory is barely four years old, that the first settlers were of that migratory class who have neither home nor family, and that women and children are but just beginning to form an appreciable percentage of the population. On the approach of winter, many whose summer exertions have returned a profit, and who, likewise, are unwilling to endure the comparative stagnation of the cold season, emigrate either to the east or west. Returning spring, however, brings back as many if not more than departed, eager to begin or to renew the toilsome yet fascinating pursuit of the gold hunter.

PHYSICAL GEOGRAPHY.—The most prominent feature of the physical geography of the Territory, particularly in the western or ore-bearing regions, is the gentleness of the acclivities and the absence of sharply projecting volcanic peaks. To the traveller passing over the summit of the Rocky mountains, on the road hither from Utah, this fact is vividly impressed upon his attention, as forming a most striking contrast to the enormous outflow of basaltic lava extending from Port Neuf cañon, in Idaho, more than 200 miles, quite to the crests of the main chain. We observe, also, even on the highest of the hills, great strata of washed and rounded boulders, loosely bound together by a granitic detritus. We find, further, quite high up on the mountains, lakes of greater or less extent, whose formation was evidently owing to the blocking up of some primeval gorge by means of glacier-borne boulders. Indeed, in one of the valleys tributary to the Deer Lodge the former location of such a lake is plainly visible. Here, for centuries perhaps, the pent-up waters, swollen by the annual melting of the winter's snows, had, year by year, further insinuated themselves into the opposing dike, until, with a mightier effort, they swept downwards to the plain, and piled up in long ridges the rocks and earthy matters in their pathway.

As might be anticipated, these hyperborean regions were once the scene of long-continued and wide-spread glacial action, the evidences of which are perfectly palpable. A locality of particular interest in this regard is the cañon of Rattlesnake creek, which takes its rise in the Bald mountain, northwest of the town of Argenta, in Beaver Head county. Here there are exposed upon the surface great slabs of quartzite, polished to the smoothness of glass, with fine parallel striations marking the course of the glaciers. At a point about half a mile below the town a large mass of this rock appears, which is remarkable for its brilliant, deep mahogany color and perfect polish.

The lower ranges and foot-hills of the Rocky mountains are made up almost entirely of rounded, rolling hills, having a substratum of drift and covered with a rich alluvium. They afford conclusive evidence of the vast and continuous wearing effect, not only of the primeval glaciers, but also of the melting snows and rains which for centuries on centuries have swept downwards from the main range.

Some very fine examples of morains are to be seen in the vicinity of Diamond City, on the eastern side of the Missouri. Great boulders of granite, worn and rounded by the attrition of the ice field, are piled up at a considerable distance from their original resting place.

Another phenomenon referable to masses of ice is to be observed in most of the larger rivers : the shallower streams, during the intense cold of the winter, become frozen to the very bottom, and envelope in a coating of ice many small and occasionally very large fragments of rock; the great increments, caused by the melting of the snows on the mountains, carry down numerous blocks of ice and the adhering stones. These latter are ultimately deposited in the river's bed, forming rapids, shoals, &c., or adding to those already formed, and still further complicating a navigation sufficiently difficult from shiftings of the line of the channel and from snags and sawyers.

The low lands furnish admirable sites for farming purposes, while the high plateaus are covered with a luxuriant growth of grasses, affording an almost limitless expanse of pasturage. Until within a very recent period, and before the hand of civilization had begun to seize the country for its own, vast herds of elk and buffalo found a lavish sustenance on the countless hills and valleys, untrod by other than Indians and a few of the hardy race of trappers.

For the purpose of description it is preferable to treat separately of the eastern and western portions of the Territory. The former, bordering on Dacota, is drained by the Missouri and Yellowstone rivers and their numerous tributaries, and is, excepting the bottom lands through which the streams flow, comparatively unknown. From such information, however, as is available, we are justified in adopting the conclusion that it is composed of rolling terrace and elevated table lands. The west, on the contrary, is mountainous.

The hill country, made up of the primitive and secondary rocks, is the habitus of the ore-bearing veins; whereas the low lands, comprising, geologically speaking, more recent sedimentary and drift formations, are prolific of useful rather than precious minerals. Below Fort Benton, the head of navigation, on the Missouri river, and likewise on the Yellowstone, after it leaves the mountains we find these water deposits, consisting of clays and sandstones, after towering far above the river banks.

Both valley systems and their subsidiary gorges are due to the eroding action of the streams draining through countless ages from off the eastern flanks of the Rocky mountains. In the eddies and lake-like depressions of these vast sedimentary plains the primeval forests, washed from their mountain fastnesses, have piled trunk on trunk to the formation of very extensive coal beds, again to be covered up by subsequent deposits of clays and sandstones. In many places along the river banks of both these streams great beds of coal and layers of sand stone, in color a dirty gray or yellow, are now plainly visible, still occupying the same hori zontal positions in which they were originally deposited.

The mountains of the Territory are, as before stated, predominant in the west. They comprise the Rocky mountain chain and its subordinate ranges, the Coeur d'Alene and Bitter Root mountains, &c., &c., forming a portion of the backbone of the continent, and covering a tract of country from 300 to 400 miles wide. Within these limits are many spurs surpassing in altitude the peaks of the main range. They give rise to numberless valleys, generally connected together by low passes. Below Fort Benton, and in the upper central portion of the Territory, between the Missouri and Milk rivers. we find two considerable upheavals, viz : the Bear's Paw, running nearly north and south, and the Little Rocky mountains, having an east and west trend. Again, nearly in the geographical centre, we find the Belt and Judith mountains, and in the south centre the Big Horn mountains, which pass out of the Territory southwardly into Dakota.

Montana is a country pre-eminently well watered. It embraces within its confines for a distance of 300 miles the entire eastern and part of the western water-shed of the Rocky mountains. Draining the former, we have the great rivers Missouri and Yellowstone. Tributary to and forming the first named, we find the Jefferson, Madison, and Gallatin, whose waters, drawn from the far western snowy peaks, unite almost simultaneously in the neighborhood of Gallatin City. Thence flowing unitedly in a northeast course they debouch into the foot-hills through a precipitous gorge, denominated by Lewis and Clarke "the gate of the mountains." Below Fort Benton the Marias, Judith, Muscleshell, and Milk rivers, draining the northern and central regions, unite with the Missouri. The Yellowstone, which with its affluents, Clark's Fork, Pryor's Fork, Big Horn, Tongue, and Powder rivers, drains the southern and southeastern portions, flows east and northeast, until, near the territorial limits, in the vicinity of Fort Union, it unites to swell the volume of waters borne by the Missouri to the Gulf of Mexico.

West of the main ridge the Hell Gate, Missoula, and Big Blackfoot rivers, flowing nearly north-northwest, unite to form the Bitter Root, which, joining with the Flat Head further north, forms the Lewis Fork of the Columbia river, whose waters find their way to the Pacific ocean.

There is but one considerable body of fresh water within the territorial limits, viz: the Flat Head lake, situated in the northwestern corner, on the western slope of the mountains, and forming the chief source of the Flat Head river above mentioned. Lying like great troughs between the moutain ridges, and drained by the principal rivers and their countless minor tributaries, we find five grand basins, and numberless subsidiary valleys; four to the east, and one west of the Rocky mountains.

The query may seem pertinent as to the motive for including in Montana rather than in Idaho the strip of territory west of the main chain. In answer it may be stated that the passes from east to west over or through the main ridge are more numerous, and in general lower and less liable to be blocked up by snow than those of the Bitter Root and Coeur d'Alene ranges. Hence for all practical purposes this magnificent valley system belongs to Montana on the east.

This western basin, with a general course of north 40° west, conformably to the trend of the main range, is made up of eight well-defined valleys. These are separated from one another by projecting spurs, over whose foot-hills there is an easy communication at all seasons of the year. Through each and all of them there flow streams prolific of trout. Near the sources of these brooks and rivers, and in general over the entire western slope, we find a luxuriant growth of pine, fir, spruce, and cedar, affording a marked contrast to the comparatively sparcely timbered east.

The theory which seems most plausible to account for this difference, which is palpable to the most unobservant when passing over the summit towards the west is, that the winds from the far southwest, warmed by a more genial sun, and absorbing the moisture evaporated over the immense expanse of the Pacific ocean, pour down, to nourish the trees and grasses, copious showers of rain, which are set free by a contact, with the colder strata about the summits of the mountains. The same winds depositing there the greater proportion of their moisture in the form of snow, have naturally a smaller amount of rain for the foot-hills and plains of the eastern slopes. The melting, however, of the heavy snow-fall carries down a rich granitic detritus, and supplies an enormous yet varying increment to the numerous tributaries to the Missouri.

Eastward of the main ridge, and stretching along the northern confines through 10°, quite to the territorial limits, and unbroken by any considerable superficial inequalities, except the Bear's Paw and Little Rocky mountains, we find the long valley drained by the Marias and Milk rivers. The upper edge of this basin is embraced within the British possessions. The major portion consists of high plateaus, rolling prairie and barren clay table lands, denominated by the trappers and French "voyageurs" "Les Manvaises Terres," or Bad Lands. These formations, barren and desolate, consist of terrace piled on terrace, marking the limits of the great sedimentary waves which have poured downwards from the mountains. Where such occur we find little or no timber, excepting along the river bottoms, which are scantily supplied with a meagre growth of cottonwood trees. The rivers have worn their pathway through these deposits, and the traveller first becomes aware of their existence when, standing upon the edge of some precipitous chasm, he observes the running waters hundreds of feet below him. Only along the immediate foot-hills are to be found sufficient timber and alluvium to invite settlement and cultivation.

Nearly in the centre of the Territory, and almost encircled by the Bear's Paw and Little Rocky mountains on the north and the Belt and Judith mountains on the south, we find a considerable basin drained by the Missouri and its tributaries, the Arrow, Judith, and Muscleshell rivers, all of which flow from south to north. A large proportion of this region may properly be embraced in the designation "bad lands." They find their most prominent exemplification from the mouth of the Judith river nearly as far as Fort Benton. Interspersed among these barren clay terraces we find most curious sandstone formations eroded, by the action of the elements, into strange and fantastic resemblances to time-worn battlements and hoary ruins. This basin is fairly watered, and although it contains a large proportion of worthless land, is not so uniformly uninviting as the preceding section.

To the east and southeast, and forming very nearly one-fourth of the Territory, we have the very extensive Big Horn valley, drained by the Yellowstone and its numerous tributaries. Less is positively known of this region than of any other portion of Montana. Hunters and trappers report the existence of wonderful falls and rapids on the upper portions of the main stream, and beautiful lakes near its source. We have, further, the descriptions of Lewis and Clark, who for 15 days, some 60 years ago, floated down its current, and also of a few venturesome voyagers of more recent periods. None, however, treat specially of other than the terrain bordering the river. The prevailing formation is evidently sedimentary drift, through which the rivers have cut their pathway. It is a country as yet sacred to the buffalo, and is pre-eminently difficult to explore owing to the determined hostility of the savages.

There is remaining the fan-like valley system above the "Gate of the Mountains," drained by the Upper Missouri and its three forks, the Jefferson, Gallatin, and Madison. This region, comprising a section of country less than 150 miles square, in area about twice the size of the State of Maryland, is emphatically Montana. Quite in the heart of the mountains, well watered and interspersed with fertile valleys and rolling grass-covered hills, it contains the chief centres of population, the most prolific placers, and a wide expanse of as yet but partially developed quartz leads. Here we find the streams draining to the east and northeast from off the eastern water-shed of the Rocky mountains. The bottom lands produce abundantly the hardier cereals and vegetables, while the hills furnish a limitless pasturage. On the mountains and high lands, where the vein mines are to be sought, the winters are long and of great severity. In many of the valleys, on the contrary, the snow falls so seldom and to such an insignificant depth that horses and cattle are able to subsist during the cold season without shelter and without care. The climate is particularly healthful, and the rare pure air of these elevated regions—the lowest being some thousands of feet above the sea level—conduces to both bodily and mental vigor.

GEOLOGY.—It is impossible at present to more than generally outline the main geological features of Montana. The want of a thorough scientific investigation of its mineral resources is just beginning to be felt, and as a knowledge of mines and mining becomes wider spread among the community, there will be a more persistent call for such surveys, and a better appreciation of the significance of the primary and secondary rocks as distinguished from drift and sedimentary deposits.

As already intimated, the formations of the Territory are marked by distinctive features in the east and west. We may dismiss a consideration of the former as connected with useful deposits other than carboniferous. The bad lands of these districts are prolific of fossils, petrifactions, &c., and afford an exhaustless and, as yet, unworked field of investigation for pure science. Drift and alluvium, spread over a wide expanse of low, rolling hills, terraces, and prairie, unbroken by other than occasional outcrops of sandstone, make up the majority of the east. The west, on the contrary, prolific of veins and placers, consists in the main of granite. The waters and glaciers have, likewise, given rise to very extensive gravel deposits merging into conglomerates of greater or less compactness. In the superficial inequalities of the mountains we find clay schists evidently of comparatively recent formation. Gneiss, mica shist, quartzite, pitchstone, and graywacke, likewise occur as subordinate local peculiarities. Talcose and reddish silicious slates, slightly charged with copper, and syenitic granite bearing gold are to be found in the mining regions. But most prominently as an ore-bearer, being, with granite, almost universal, we find large masses of blue, yellow, and occasionally whitish metamorphic limestone of a distinctly chrystalline structure and highly magnesian. This rock occurs apparently as an intercallation between dikes of quartzite and the grand granitic substratum of the country. It forms a species of mineral belt, disconnected, however, and generally in each district of limited extent.

Montana is rich in fossils, and hence the geologic age of the various formations admit of a reasonably easy determination. Aside from the above-mentioned prolific bad lands, there occurs near the summit of the range back of Virginia City a very heavy deposit of fossil shells. Individual specimens from this source are to be met with both on the surface and in the placer washings lower down the mountain, at that point where Alder gulch begins. Professor Swallow, State geologist of Missouri and Kansas, discovered a locality of fossils in the vicinity of the copper mines at the head of the Muscleshell river, which is so denominated from the great abundance of fresh water muscle shells found on its banks. I myself collected quite a number of fossils from the clay schists of Birch and Grasshopper creeks, in Beaver Head county, which, through the kindness of Dr. Blatchley, have been handed for determination to Professor Whitney, State geologist of California. The finest specimen was presented to me by a Mr. Taylor, residing near Bannock. It consisted of the lower jaw, incisors, and molars of some medium-sized graminivorous animal, and was in a particularly fine state of preservation. The fossil bore some resemblance to the teeth of a mountain sheep, an animal which, through uninterrupted pursuit, is fast becoming extinct. The fossils from Birch creek consisted entirely of the remains of shell fish. There was reported, in 1865, the discovery of the head bones and the skeleton of a buffalo, almost entire. They were found in Grizzly gulch, near Helena, lying immediately upon the bed rock, and covered up to a depth of 40 to 45 feet with wash gravel and alluvium. In the same year also there was discovered, on Meagher bar, opposite the town of Nevada, in Alder gulch, the lower jaw-bone of a member of the human family, measuring five inches from point to point of the condyles. An inferior maxillary of these dimensions would indicate some giant individual of an extinct species from $10\frac{1}{2}$ to 12 feet in height. At the same time and place there was found an enormous fossil tooth, six inches long, four inches wide, and between eight and nine inches from the crown through to the lower portions of the root. Mr. T. H. Kleinschmidt, of Helena, has in his possession two enormous fossil teeth, exhumed, some two years since, from the wash gravel of Grizzly gulch.

The discovery of these fossils in the gold-bearing drift of Montana adds another link to the chain of evidence confirmatory of the truth of the statements of Professor Whitney, State geologist of California, as to the age of the placers. They show conclusively that their formation here in Montana was either coincident with, or but little subsequent to, the advent of the mammalia, and that some of them may have been deposited even as late as the age of man. These exuviæ of extinct species of animals are preserved with the greatest difficulty, not only on account of their facility of crumbling on exposure to the air, but also from the apathy of the finders, who regard them curiously for the moment and then cast them aside into the neglected corners of their cabins.

MINING REGIONS.—Under this designation we embrace all placer deposits, both the superficial detrital formations and the deep-lying conglomerate-like cement diggings, as well as the infiltrated system of quartz veins. In general terms, we may designate both slopes of the Rocky mountains as pertaining to the mining regions.

The crests of the main chain, from the point of entering the Territory until reaching Mullan's Pass, in about latitude 46¼° and longitude 35° west of Washington, maintain a course very nearly north 40° west. From this locality they make a sharp turn to the southwest, and run on thus until they pass into Idaho. Within this limit the ridge is cut through in but one place by the far western affluents of the Big Hole branch of the Jefferson river.

We find on the eastern slope two belts of ore-bearing country resembling an inverted V, the apex of which is towards the north. The left hand belt starts from Horse prairie below Bannock City, in the southwest; thence passes through Blue Wing, Argenta, and an eastern system parallel to the Silver Bow and Butte City districts on the west, and continues onward through Beavertown, Jefferson City, Helena, and Silver City, northwards. The second belt commences high up in the mountains south of Virginia City; passes thence northerly through Ramshorn, Brandon, &c., then disappears or gives but faint traces of its presence in the alluvial valley through which passes the river Jefferson, and shows itself again near Beavertown, from whence the two eastern belts pass northwardly as one.

West of the crests of the main range we find not only less developed but also less continuous zones of impregnation. That the points of enrichment appear to be more isolated is owing, doubtless, to a less thorough prospecting. Further south, and drained by the westernmost affluent of the Big Hole—emptying its waters, it is true, to the east, but from its position preferably credited to the west—we find the rich but shallow diggings centring about French gulch, a locality long since worked over and abandoned.

Advancing northwardly we have a mineral belt just west of the crests of the main chain, at the head of the Blackfoot river, running nearly northwest and southeast, conformably to the trend of the mountains and corresponding to a western prolongation of the mineral belt of Silver Bow and Butte City.

We find still another belt southward of, and having a marked parallelism with, the general course of the Hell Gate river, bearing about west-northwest and east-southeast. This belt embraces Gold creek, the point where gold was first discovered, and likewise its continuation on the head-waters of Flint creek, where, lately, there was reported the discovery of valuable gold-bearing quartz lodes. Hence, pursuing the same direction, we still find evidences of gold deposits on most of the affluents emptying into the Hell Gate further west.

The most recent attraction for the migratory, restless race of miners, is a point on the western slope of the mountains far towards the northwest, and only a few miles distant from the line of the British possessions. The particular locality is said to be between the Jocko mission and Thompson's river, where there are believed to be both rich and extensive deposits forming those species of placer mines known as gulch and bar diggings. Many people have flocked thither, both from Montana and from the neighboring Territories. So great, indeed, has been the exodus from certain localities that many mining camps are entirely deserted. Whether the reported richness will be borne out by a closer examination remains to be proven. Such migrations are of too common occurrence in the history of placer mining to merit more than passing mention, except for the purpose of exemplifying a peculiar phase of life in the mountains. Washings yielding fair average returns are abandoned on the instant so soon as the whispered rumor spreads abroad that fabulous richness lies hidden on the bed rock of some far-off ravine. The tireless prospector dares wind and snow in the depth of winter to hunt up new placers, and seems to prefer such as are most inaccessible and most dangerous to explore on account of hostile Indians. On the approach of winter these "stampedes," as they are called, occur most frequently. The summer has yielded its harvests, favorable to some, but unfavorable to many, and winter begins to lock up for a six months' rest the watercourses which are indispensable to placer mining. Hence, the prospector, unable longer to continue his washings, starts forth to renew the chase of fortune, laden only with pick, pan, and shovel, and an amount of provisions measured by the length of his purse or the soundness of his credit. Sometimes in company, but more frequently solitary and alone, they carefully investigate such ravines, gulleys, &c., as experience or fancy may dictate. Buoyed up by the hope of ultimately "striking it rich," they endure every species of hardship and privation and not unfrequently are frozen to death. Amputations of frost-bitten hands and feet are of quite common occurrence.

This nomadic instinct, combined with practiced observation, alacrity in every emergency, and self-reliant bravery, has moulded a race of hardy pioneers, fit instruments to subdue the wilderness and the mountain-fastnesses. To such men are due the discovery of new mining regions in localities where no inducement other than the yellow dust will draw tho white man. They pave the way for oncoming civilization, and leave to others the fairest fruits of their toils and privations. As soon as their old camping grounds become comparatively settled and self-sustaining, these children of the frontier seek other ranges and wilder solitudes. Every fall and winter are marked by countless minor excitements and one or more gigantic stampedes, depopulating entire districts.

Up to the summer and fall of 1865 these migratory movements were in the main confined to a comparatively circumscribed area, comprising what now constitutes the settled portion of the Territory,

The superficial placers having at this time begun to show symptoms of exhaustion, naturally gave rise to investigations of more distant localities. In January, 1866, a rush took place to the mouth of Sun river towards a point some 60 miles from Fort Benton. As a result no diggings of any value were discovered and a large number of the deluded enthusiasts were frozen to death. In July, of the same year, the placers of Little Blackfoot, Nevada gulch, and the Hell Gate country, all on the western slopes, attracted considerable attention, and remain until the present time a region of undiminished interest. In the following month of August there sprung up an intense excitement caused by the report of fabulously rich placers in the neighborhood of Fort Lemhi, in the Salmon river country of Idaho. In the same month a large number made their way to the Wind River mountains of Dakota, west and southwest of the extreme southern sources of the Yellowstone. Neither of these excitements appears to have justified expectation. That to Salmon river continued through the winters of 1866–'67. Thousands were drawn thither, and others kept pouring in until the disappearance of the snow late in the spring so far exposed the ground as emphatically to disprove the illusion. Men remained for many months exposed to the cruelties of a very severe winter, built up a large town, held unprospected claims at enormous figures, and at length abandoned the country in disgust, condemning as fiercely as they had previously unreasonably lauded it. In October also of 1866, a stampede of some magnitude was directed to the Saskatchawan country, 650 miles north of Helena and in the British possessions. No diggings of importance rewarded the prospectors.

No permanent prosperity and no fixed centres of population are possible until such time as the superficial placers have ceased to yield a prolific booty of easy extraction. The long rows of deserted habitations, once teeming with the busy life of a flourishing mining town, bear melancholy testimony to the inefficiency of the placers alone to lay the foundations of permanent towns and cities. The real prosperity of a mining country may be dated from the time when the majority of the gulches, bars, &c., are worked out, since, at such time, the people are compelled to turn their attention to the quartz veins, which alone promise permanency and a lasting source of revenue to well-directed enterprise. That many adventures terminate unfortunately; that vast sums are wasted through folly and ignorance, so culpable as almost to deserve to be branded as criminal, is not to be wondered at. The art of mining and the fundamental principles of metallurgy, as applied to the North American mineral regions, are of too recent formation to be, even in their general outlines, at all widely spread amongst the people. Hence, dazzled by a pursuit having as its immediate object the representatives of value in all civilized nations, viz., gold and silver, the majority of men lose sight of those primal economical considerations which no individual of practical business sense ever neglects or overlooks. They begin, not by counting the cost, but by rearing brilliant imaginary superstructures on a very meagre substratum of fact, and hence the magnificent proportions of the imposing edifice are in constant jeopardy from the faintest breathings of hard facts and common-sense reality.

Such opinions, the result of ignorance and malappreciation, must still continue until those men whose lives are devoted solely to the acquirement of a practical acquaintance with mining affairs shall have impressed upon the great body of the community the fundamental maxims necessary to successful mining. These may be summed up briefly as follows: First, a reasonably large estimate of cost; and, secondly, a just estimate of the average working yield by such process, either amalgamation or smelting, as may be determined upon by a reliable and competent authority. Undue haste in erecting mills and machinery before a sufficient degree of development is apparent, has been, more than any other cause, the fruitful source of failure and disappointment. Companies organized with an insufficient working capital, and blunderingly conducted, find their resources failing them precisely at the moment when most needed, and many mining adventures thus prove failures even when the mine itself is of real value.

DISTRIBUTION OF THE VARIOUS METALS AND MINERALS.—There seems to be no marked segregation from one another of the gold, silver, copper, or coal bearing localities, other than that the last mentioned is found mainly in the sedimentary formations of the east. Indeed, the phenomenon of double veins, so called, namely, those having pure smelting ores, as galenas, oxides and carbonates of lead on the one wall, and amalgamable noble silver minerals, as silver glance, stephanite, dark and light ruby silver, &c, &c., on the other, are of not uncommon occurrence. Gold is found over a wide extent of country, the main development of which, up to the present time, has been expended on placer deposits. Vein mining both for gold and silver is just beginning to come prominently into notice. Gold quartz of greater or less promise has been found in the immediate vicinity of all the localities once celebrated for their placers, viz: near Bannock, Virginia City, Helena City, Highland, &c., &c. Silver ores suitable for smelting are found in the Blue Wing and Argenta districts in the southwest, also in the vicinity of Jefferson City, in several of the districts near Helena, and in some of the mines of Flint creek and Mill creek. Silver ores suitable for amalgamation are found in Brown's gulch, in the neighborhood of Virginia City, and across the range in Deer Lodge county, on one of the branches of Flint creek, at Phillipsburg, &c., &c.

Copper ores, of such as carry a predominating percentage of this metal, are found among the eastern foot-hills, near the sources of the Muscleshell river, also in the valley of the Prickly Pear, and west of the range near Butte City. Traces of this metal are found in nearly all the mining districts, and a most curious formation of a true copper placer is observable near Beavertown, a short distance south of Jefferson City. The particles of pure copper, pointed, yet apparently uncrystallized, seem, in this instance, to be held together by a species of quartzy detritus.

We find, also, clays and sandstones superimposed and underlying the coal beds in those places where the local peculiarities of the surface have proved favorable to sedimentary and drift formations—that is, mainly, as before stated, in the east, but likewise among the foot-hills and, in one or two well-known instances, quite high up on the mountains of the west.

CENTRES OF POPULATION.—The chief centres of population in the Territory are three, viz: Bannock, Virginia and Helena cities. The motive of their foundation was the extent and profitableness of the placer deposits in their immediate vicinity. And since the limit of productiveness of the superficial placers may be determined to a degree of reasonable exactness, it is necessary to establish a claim to other local resources in order to maintain in the future the relative pre-eminence of the past.

First in the order of settlement we find Bannock City, formerly called East Bannock, in contradistinction to another town of the same name lying to the southwest, and then likewise in the Territory of Idaho. The diggings were discovered in the summer of 1862 by one John White, from Colorado. The town is situated in a narrow gorge in the midst of a series of rolling hills. Through it there flows a considerable stream of water, called Willard's or Grasshopper creek, which is a tributary to one of the three chief affluents of the Jefferson river. Considerable mining was done the year of discovery. The majority of the claims paid well and uniformly without any surprisingly rich yields. The gold produced was of a very high rate of fineness, coining $19 50 per ounce. One particularly clean and choice lot, of upwards of $20,000, taken from a single claim, coined the very unusual sum of a few cents over $20 per ounce; that is very nearly as much as pure gold, which is valued at $20 67 per ounce. The placer deposits are still an object of pursuit, although the main reliance in the future must be the vein mines opposite to and below the town. The rocks of the vicinity are granite and metamorphic limestone, carrying the ore-bearing quartz lodes. We find some quartzite, and above the town clays and sandstones, with a considerable deposit of alluvium along the immediate borders of the creek.

The first territorial legislature assembled here, and among its other enactments promulgated a series of laws determining the method of location, record, tenure, &c., of lode claims. These laws, although in the main modelled after the miner's customs of Idaho, which were in force up to and for some months subsequent to the date of segregation therefrom of Montana, were, nevertheless, altered in several minor and one or more fundamental points. The Idaho legislature did not attempt by statutory enactment to define the rights, privileges and penalties of the miners, but, according to the civil practice act, permitted to be brought in evidence "proof of the customs, usages or regulations established and in force in the mining districts, embracing such claims and such customs, usages or regulations, when not in conflict with the laws of the Territory, shall govern the decision of the action." (Civil Practice Act, sec. 576.) As showing the animus of the framers, and the opinions in vogue in Montana at this period, it may not be inadmissible to insert these laws here.

We may premise by stating that these mid-continental Territories are stamped with the impress of Colorado. From geographical contiguity, and the fact that the bulk of the early immigration found its way hither from the east, it is only to be expected that the mining legislation should show unmistakable evidences of its origin, and hence be clearly distinguishable from that of the west. A comparison of the two systems, in many respects fundamentally at variance, will be touched upon hereafter.

AN ACT relating to the discovery of gold and silver quartz leads, lodes, or ledges, and of the manner of their location. (Approved December 26, 1864.)

Be it enacted by the legislative assembly of the Territory of Montana, That any person who may hereafter discover any quartz lead, lode, or ledge, shall be entitled to one claim thereon by right of discovery, and one claim each by pre-emption.

SEC. 2. That in order to entitle any person or persons to record in the county recorder's office of the proper county, any lead, lode, or ledge, either of gold or silver, or claim thereon, there shall first be discovered on said lead, lode, or ledge a vein or crevice of quartz or ore, with at least one well-defined wall.

SEC. 3. Claims on any lead, lode, or ledge, either of gold or silver, hereafter discovered, shall consist of not more than 200 feet along the lead, lode, or ledge, together with all dips, spurs, and angles emanating or diverging from said lead, lode, or ledge, as also 50 feet on each side of said lead, lode, or ledge, for working purposes: *Provided,* That when two or more leads, lodes, or ledges shall be discovered within 100 feet of each other, either running parallel or crossing each other, the ground between such leads, lodes, or ledges shall belong equally to the claimants of said leads, lodes, or ledges, without regard to priority of discovery or pre-emption.

SEC. 4. When any leads, lodes, or ledges shall cross each other, the quartz, ore, or mineral in the crevice or vein at the place of crossing shall belong to and be the property of the claimants upon the lead, lode, or ledge first discovered.

SEC. 5. That before any record shall be made, under the provisions of this act, there shall be placed at each extremity of the discovered claim a good and substantial stake, not less than five inches in diameter, said stake to be firmly planted or sunken in the ground, extending two feet above the ground; that upon each stake there shall be placed, in legible characters, the name of the lead, lode, or ledge, and that of the discoverer or discoverers, the date of discovery, and the name of each pre-emptor or claimant, and the direction or bearing, as near as may be, of his or her claim; said stake and the inscription thereon to be replaced at least once in twelve months by the claimants on said leads, lodes, or ledges, if torn down or otherwise destroyed.

Sec. 6. Notice of the discovery or pre-emption upon any lead, lode, or ledge shall be filed for record in the county recorder's office, of the county in which the same may be situated, within fifteen days of the date of the discovery or pre-emption; and there shall at the same time be an oath taken before the recorder that the claimant or claimants are each and all of them bona fide residents of the Territory of Montana; and there shall be deposited in the recorder's office, either by the discoverer or some pre-emptor, a specimen of the quartz, ore, or mineral extracted or taken from said lead, lode, or ledge, which said specimen shall be properly labelled by the recorder and preserved in his office.

Sec. 7. That any person or persons who shall take up or destroy, or cause the same to be done, any of the said stakes, or who shall in anywise purposely deface or obliterate any part or portion of the writing or inscription placed thereon, shall be deemed guilty of a misdemeanor, and upon conviction thereof before any court of competent jurisdiction, shall be punished by a fine of not more than $1,000 or imprisonment in the county jail not more than 90 days, or by both such fine and imprisonment.

Sec. 8. That the amount of ground which may be taken up upon any lead, lode, or ledge, in addition to the discovery claim, shall be limited to 1,000 feet along said lead, lode, or ledge in each direction from the discovery claim thereon.

Sec. 9. All lead, lode, or ledge claims, taken up and recorded in pursuance with the provisions of this act, shall entitle the person recording to hold the same to the use of himself, his heirs and assigns; and conveyances of quartz claims shall hereafter require the same formalities and shall be subject to the same rules of construction as the transfer and conveyance of real estate.

Sec. 10. That if at any time previous to the passage of this act, claims have been taken up and recorded in the recorder's office of the proper county, upon any actual or proper lead, lode, or ledge of quartz, ore, or mineral, the owners or proper claimants of said respective claim shall hold the same to the use of themselves, their heirs and assigns.

Sec. 11. That the act relating to the discovery of gold and silver quartz lodes and the manner of their location, passed by the Idaho legislature and approved February 4, 1864, and all other acts, or parts of acts, inconsistent with this act, be, and the same are hereby, repealed.

Sec. 12. This act shall take effect from and after this date.

Again, by an act approved January 17, 1865, it was enacted that quartz mining claims and water rights "shall become part and parcel of the county records, and shall be evidence in any court or courts of competent jurisdiction;" thus placing the titles to quartz claims on the same footing and making their transfer subject to the same formalities as those to real property.

The next great discovery, viz., that of Alder creek, in the present county of Madison, was the motive to the foundation of Virginia City, and the minor towns of Summit, Highland, Nevada, Central, and Junction. This gulch was the richest and longest ever worked in Montana, and probably in the world, being nearly 20 miles in length, and uniformly productive throughout by far the greater portion. The creek flowing through it received its name from the thick growth of alders once lining its banks, of which at present no twig nor root remains. It takes its rise among the snows of the bald mountain south of the mining hamlet called Summit City, and discharges its waters into the Passamari, or Stinking Water river, one of the tributaries to the Jefferson.

The history of the discovery of the gulch was substantially as follows: In the spring of 1863 there started out from Bannock, on a prospecting tour northwards, a party composed of the following individuals: Wm. Fairweather, Thos. Cover, B. Hughes, H. Edgar, L. Simonds, G. Orr, Wm. Sweeney, and H. Rodgers. Having journeyed as far as the Deer Lodge valley they concluded to alter their course, and, leaving Orr behind, they made their way to the Yellowstone country. Here they fell into the hands of a large party of Crow Indians, who relieved them of nearly all their provisions, and at the same time exchanged horses with them. During the night all except Simonds managed to make good their escape; they travelled as rapidly as possible, without halting to prospect, and, worn out with fatigue, camped on the east side of the stream since known as Alder creek.

Wm. Fairweather crossed over the stream, and on examining the locality observed a point where the bed rock lay exposed above the surface. He returned to the camping ground, and in the company of Edgar went to prospect the bar. The first panful of earth yielded $1 75, and after superficially testing other points, in all of which they obtained encouraging prospects, four of the party proceeded formally to stake their claims. Fairweather, Edgar, Cover, and Hughes marked out four claims on what was afterwards known as the Fairweather bar. They likewise secured for themselves four claims on Cover's bar. Rodgers and Sweeney staked off two claims, one on each bar named after themselves, and one on the Cover bar. Being without provisions the party hurried back to Bannock City, from whence returning in company of their friends, the gulch was staked off on the 6th and 7th of June, 1863.

Within the space of less than two years Alder gulch contained five thriving towns besides Virginia, an incorporated city containing nearly 10,000 inhabitants.

This Virginia City, Montana, must not be confounded with Virginia City, Nevada, distant some 800 miles on an air line to the southwest.

At the head of the gulch, far back upon the mountains and nine miles south of the city, the gold found in the washings was coarse, and many nuggets were picked up varying in value from $200 to $800. A short distance below the town of Summit the gold appeared in the form of flat rounded plates, known as scale gold, and the further one removed down stream the finer did the dust appear, until it consisted almost entirely of the finest particles, known as flour gold. During 1863, the year of discovery, but few of the richest claims were opened and explored. This was owing to the fact that the pay stratum lay deep, and hence arose the necessity for unity of action on the part of the owners of contiguous claims in order to carry out a systematic plan of bed-rock drainage. The following year, however, saw the full development of this most remarkable gulch.

No better exemplification of the spirit of the miners and their peculiar customs can be offered than a study of the district rules and regulations for the government of placer claims. As proving a good example of their kind, and containing a reasonably clear and concise statement of the wishes and rights of the miners as expressed by themselves, we have the following regulations of Alder gulch. These laws were drafted by a select committee chosen at a meeting of the miners *en masse;* the motive to which is contained in the following preamble:

Whereas the laws now in force in Fairweather district, Madison county, Montana Territory, have proved insufficient to protect the rights of the miners of said district;

And whereas the rights and interests of the miners of the district are of such a nature as not to admit of a resort to the tedious remedy of the ordinary process of law for every violation of those rights:

Now, therefore, we, the miners of said district, in public meeting assembled, in pursuance of legal notice, for the purpose of defending our rights and duties, and the protection of our several interests, do hereby resolve and declare that the rules and provisions following shall be the law of Fairweather district from the date of enactment, viz: September 16, 1864.

ARTICLE A.

SECTION 1. Hereafter the officers of the district shall consist of a president and secretary, who shall hold their offices for the term of six months, and until their successors are duly elected and enter upon the discharge of the duties of their office.

SEC. 2. It shall be the duty of the president to call a meeting of the miners of the district at any time on the written application of five claimholders of the district, of which he shall give three days' notice previous to the day of meeting, by three written or printed advertisements put at three of the most public places in the district, and he shall preside at each meeting.

SEC. 3. It shall be the duty of the secretary to attend all meetings called by the president, and keep a true record of the proceedings thereof, and file the same with the county recorder; and he shall preside at all meetings when the president is absent.

SEC. 4. After suit commenced in any case wherein the title to a claim is called in question, neither party shall be held liable to represent said claim during the pendency of litigation, but the same shall be deemed to be represented in favor of the real owner by operation of law.

SEC. 5. Every person shall be entitled to hold, by pre-emption, one creek, bar, or hill claim, and as many of either kind by purchase as he shall represent, according to the laws of the district.

SEC. 6. Any co-partnership or company of persons shall be entitled to hold the same number of claims by pre-emption and purchase as the number of persons comprising such co-partnership or company would be entitled to hold in their individual capacity.

SEC. 7. The lessee of a claim (if he shall have agreed to completely work out the same, and his lease be recorded) shall be entitled to hold one claim by pre-emption, and his work done on the leased claim represented by him.

SEC. 8. No person who, having pre-empted a claim by recording thereon, has forfeited the same, or who has failed to receive a good title thereto, or who shall in good faith sell and convey the same, shall be thereby debarred from holding another claim by pre-emption.

SEC. 9. Every claim shall be considered as pre-empted upon which the pre-emptor or purchaser shall, by himself, his agent, or hired hands, perform three full days' work in each week, and such representative of each and every claim that such pre-emptor or purchaser holds in the district, provided that each and all of said claims have been duly recorded; and if any person shall represent a claim by working thereon without having his bill of sale or other conveyance thereof duly recorded, then and in that case he shall not be entitled to hold any other claim in the district, either by pre-emption or purchase, but shall be confined and limited to the claim upon which he has so worked until it is recorded.

SEC. 10. Co-partners in any company or companies, working one claim in the district, shall be considered as representing thereby all the claims held by them in the district.

SEC. 11. Any claim to which a drain ditch is commenced or beginning, if the holder of the same shall compose one of the ditch company, or shall put and continue hands at work in the same, shall be considered as duly represented until the drain ditch is completed to such claim.

SEC. 12. The absence of any person from the district shall not impair or invalidate his rights therein, provided his interests are represented by his partners or agents, or men in his employ.

SEC. 13. The rights of a sick member shall be respected during his illness, and the certificate of a physician shall be sufficient evidence of such illness.

SEC. 14. Any miner who shall have expended $600 on his claim, or who, for want of money for opening the same, is unable to represent according to law, shall have the privilege of working on any other claim in the district in order to raise money to enable him fully to open his own claim, provided he shall put up notices on his own claim, stating where he is at work, and his rights shall be respected during the time he is so at work for others.

SEC. 15. It shall and may be lawful for any person or company to dig a drain ditch through the claim or claims of any person or company, for the purpose of drainage; and any person or company making such ditch shall have a lien upon any and all such claims thoroughly drained thereby for a just and equal proportion of the cost thereof. But no lien shall be enforced until the holder of the claim affected thereby shall avail himself of the benefit of the ditch.

SEC. 16. The water in any creek or gulch shall belong exclusively to the miners of the creek or gulch.

SEC. 17. Each gulch claim shall be entitled to one sluice-head of water of not less than twenty inches—to be measured subject to a pressure of six inches, and such additional quantity as may be necessary for mining purposes, if such additional quantity be not used to the injury of the rights of others.

SEC. 18. The interest of the holder or holders of any creek or gulch claim is hereby declared to be a chattel interest, consisting of the right to the possession of the land and the water thereupon inseparable and indivisible, except by the consent of the party or parties in interest, made in due form of law, and then only to such an extent as shall not impair or infringe the rights of others.

SEC. 19. No person or persons in company shall have the right, by pre-emption or otherwise, to claim and hold an exclusive right or privilege in or to any portion of the water in any creek or gulch in the district, except as herein provided; and any ditch, pipe, channel, flume, or other means of conveyance heretofore made, or which may hereafter be made, by which the water in any creek or gulch in the district shall be directed from its original channel and carried beyond any creek or gulch claim, without leaving in the creek or gulch the quantity of water belonging to each claim, is hereby declared to be a public nuisance, and may be abated immediately, in such way and manner as shall be in accordance with the laws of this Territory and the common law of the land.

Sec. 20. All dams, flumes, embankments, or other obstructions, which shall cause tailings to accumulate, or a division of the water, to the damage of the miners above or below the same, shall be deemed public nuisances, and may be abated in the manner hereinbefore provided for other cases; and all persons injured thereby shall be entitled to recover damages of the person or persons who have created, or may create, authorize, or permit, upon his or their claims, all or any of said nuisances.

Sec. 21. No miner shall so run his tailings, or shovel or pile up the same, as to damage any claim, either above or below him.

Sec. 22. Any miner of a creek or gulch claim who shall suffer injury by the escape of water from any side ditch, shall be entitled to recover damages therefor by the ordinary process of law.

Sec. 23. It shall not be lawful for any person to place or run tailings into a side ditch made for the protection of a pit or drain ditch.

Sec. 24. Every claim not duly represented, according to the laws of the district, until the day upon which the claims in this district may at any time hereafter be laid by, shall be forfeited; and it shall be lawful for another person to record and pre-empt such forfeited claim at any time after the day on which the claims in the district shall be laid by, and before the first day of May next following.

Sec. 25. Hereafter all claims shall be deemed to be laid by during the interval between the last day of October and the first day of May of each year.

Sec. 26. All rules, laws, and regulations heretofore in this district, not conflicting with the laws, rules, and regulations herein enacted, are hereby continued in force; and all laws, rules, and regulations heretofore in force, conflicting in the least, in whole or in part, with any of the laws, rules, and regulations herein adopted, or any portion thereof, are hereby repealed.

Sec. 27. These laws shall take effect and be in force from and after this 16th day of September, A. D. 1864.

ARTICLE B.

Section 1. Bar mining claims shall consist of 100 feet up and down the gulch or creek, and running back the width of the bar.

Sec. 2. Creek claims shall be 100 feet in length, and including the bar or creek bottom and head of the stream.

Sec. 3. All discovery claims shall be safely held, whether worked or not.

Sec. 4. The centre of the creek shall be the line.

Northwardly from Virginia City we find Divin's gulch, which drains from east to west into the Passamari, a tributary to the Jefferson river. The gulch is about nine miles long, and paid well throughout nearly its entire length. A ditch was brought in from Ram's Horn creek, with a sufficient fall for the introduction of bed-rock flumes. Still further north, flowing in a like direction from the same range, we find Mill, Wisconsin, and Indian creeks, and the above-mentioned Ram's Horn creek, none of which appear to have been remarkable for placer deposits of any magnitude.

The discovery next in importance, subsequent to that of Alder gulch, was Last Chance gulch, near the site of the present city of Helena. This gulch was discovered in the summer of 1864, and the first claims were staked by a company of some 20 or 25 persons. This party, after locating claims for themselves near the point of discovery, moved further down the ravine, forming a new district, and there, likewise, staked off for themselves an equal number of pre-emptions. Subsequently a party of immigrants from Minnesota, arriving too late to proceed to Alder gulch, began prospecting in the adjacent tributary gulches, and discovered the diggings of Grizzly and Oro Fino. It was not, however, until the February of the following year that the truth in regard to its great richness became generally known. Those who had already pre-empted claims and had worked on them during the latter part of the summer satisfied prying interrogatories by replying, in the language of the miners, that "they were making grub," or, in other words, gaining nothing beyond a bare support.

The city of Helena lies on both sides of Last Chance gulch, and just above its point of junction with the valley of the Prickly Pear, an affluent to the Missouri, and on the low ridge separating Last Chance from Dry gulch, running parallel thereto. Oro Fino and Grizzly are tributary to the former, and Bowery and Tucker to the latter. In the distance north are to be seen the jagged peaks of the Bear's Teeth mountains. The hills of the immediate vicinity, however, present a series of gentle acclivities, with a considerable covering of wash.

We find near the town a very curious intermingling of limestone, sandstone, and quartzite, and on the hills back of the town a heavy body of granite, from whose quartz veins the valleys and adjacent gulches were, beyond a doubt, filled with their auriferous detritus. Helena forms the actual centre of a very extensive network of placer deposits, embracing upwards of 40 miles of greater or less richness.

The bulk of the auriferous treasure is now exhausted. Desultory mining is, it is true, still prosecuted in several of the neighboring ravines, as Last Chance, Nelson, &c. The first rude washings always leave behind them a greater or less percentage of gold, dependent upon the skill of the workers and upon the form of the dust, whether coarse or fine, the former being saved with the greater ease. The placers, once worked over, are said to be exhausted; that is, will no longer yield a profit except with cheaper labor or a more thorough and systematic method of mining. The diggings now fall into the hands of the Chinese, who patiently glean the fields abandoned by the whites; or, where the ground is favorable, it is bought up by capitalists for the purpose of a reworking by what is known as bed-rock flumes. The treasure overlooked in the first rude washings of Alder gulch and the famous Last Chance, &c., of Helena, yet await a reworking on this plan. That such has not already been done is with difficulty explainable, especially in regard to the last mentioned gulch, where 27 miles of main ditches, carrying 4,000 inches of water, miners' measurement, may be readily diverted to that end. Undertakings of this character in California and elsewhere often yield as much if not more than that obtained from the first washings.

4 T

It would be impossible to enumerate here all or even a large proportion of the gulches east of the mountains within 25 miles of the city of Helena. Portions of the same placer system extend across the Missouri river to the northeast, and others again bear away to the north as far as Silver City. All have been productive in a greater or less degree. Near their sources, as is usual, were found large masses of gold, called nuggets, and a diminishing size of grain the further we remove down stream.

The ravines in the immediate vicinity of the town were but poorly supplied with water, a want which has long since been removed by an elaborate system of flumes and ditches.

A few of the more prominent gulches may be enumerated and described, as follows:

Last Chance, the first discovered, is seven to eight miles long. In May of 1865 a drain ditch was run underneath the town to drain the bed rock of this gulch, to the more convenient extraction of the pay stratum, which averaged some 4 feet in depth by 18 feet in width.

Grizzly was remarkable in having two pay strata, the one above the other, thus proving that the sources of gold supply were tapped at two different periods, and were separated from one another by a deposit of non-auriferous wash.

Nelson, first prospected December 25, 1864, and hence called Christmas gulch, is distant from Helena eight miles, and had a narrow pay streak of remarkably high-grade gold. The auriferous dirt was found at a depth of 35 to 40 feet, after passing through a barren wash gravel. The bed rock consisted of a whitish decomposed sandstone, having upon it no large amount of water. The gulch is some six miles long, and heads near the same summit from whence issues Grizzly, and runs at right angles to the last named. Nelson gulch produced in 1865 a large and curiously shaped nugget, resembling an oyster shell, and in value $2,075.

Dry gulch, so called from the absence therein of a running stream, produced earth sufficiently rich to pay for hauling to water, a distance of one-half to one and one-half miles.

To the east, and between Helena and Montana cities, are two dry gulches, each about nine miles long, running very nearly parallel and heading in the same summit.

Across the Missouri river, some 20 miles southeast of Cañon Ferry, we find Diamond City and the famous Confederate gulch. From one of the bars of this ravine a small party of five or six men are said to have taken out in the summer of 1864 about 1,400 pounds of gold dust, in value nearly $300,000 coin. Confederate is situated nearly 35 miles east of Helena, and in that part of Gallatin county named in honor of the late General Meagher. It takes its rise in the Belt range of mountains, and pursues a southwest course for 15 miles. Diamond City, the nucleus of a very extensive series of hydraulic workings, is on Confederate gulch, six miles from its source. The bed rock consists of slate.

As tributary gulches, we find Cement, Montana, Greenhorn, Boulder, Baker, &c. Immediately above the town are the great bars called Montana and Last Chance. Four miles north of Confederate, and running parallel, we have White's gulch, and passing over the summit we arrive at Thomas's gulch.

Dismissing with this cursory description the placers to the east, we may briefly touch upon those west of the main range. The latter, amid the general impoverishment of the washings, have, during the past season, attracted more attention than any others. Prominent among these are the gulches in the vicinity of Blackfoot City, which is situated in Deer Lodge county, and distant from Helena 25 miles by the trail. Opposite to Helena, being on the other side of the range, and draining from-off the western slopes towards the west and southwest, we find the Little Blackfoot, Cottonwood, and Silver Bow creeks, which form the easternmost affluents to the Hell Gate river. These streams, with their minor tributaries, give rise to numerous gulches, of which the more important may be enumerated and described as follows: Tiger gulch, the first struck in the vicinity, was discovered by Colonel Pemberton, Hugh Bealton, and party, late in the winter of 1864. Ophir, discovered in the spring following, lies to the north of and is tributary to the Little Blackfoot. We have, further, McClellan, near Blackfoot City; Washington, west of and some 12 miles distant from Ophir; Jefferson, parallel to and two miles distant from Washington; Madison, two and a half miles northwest of Jefferson; and Carpenter's bar, some two miles east of Blackfoot City, forming a portion of a long rolling prairie. Northwardly from the last-named gulch is found a series of veins bearing away towards Snow Shoe, Deadwood, and Uncle Ben's gulches, which head near the crests of the main range. On the very highest point of this vicinity there were found dry diggings sufficiently remunerative to warrant hauling the auriferous earth a long distance to water, down the mountain. Here a nugget was found in value somewhat over $3,000 in coin. The formation of this district consists, in the main, of granite, with occasional stretches of clay slate near the base of the mountains, and occasionally a species of indurated talcose slate.

There further appears quite an extensive body of placers on the south side of the Hell Gate river, and in the mountains enclosing the valley of the Deer Lodge. Of these we may enumerate Elk creek, some 14 miles long, with a pay stratum of about four feet; Bear gulch, seven to eight miles long, with a bed rock covered up to a depth of 40 feet; also Dave's, Deep, Rock, Douglas, &c.

The placers of Silver Bow and Butte City, seven miles above, are situated, likewise, on the western slope of the southeastern extremity of the Deer Lodge valley and about 90 miles distant from Virginia City. The Silver Bow diggings were discovered in July, 1864, by a prospector named Barber. For six months subsequent thereto they attracted but little attention. The success of the Pennsylvania company, however, again brought them into notice so favorably that, as a result, claims were taken up and recorded a distance of 25 miles. The creek, especially in the lower portions, has the very insignificant fall of little more than four inches to the 100 feet, whereby the drainage is rendered difficult and a dump for the tailings almost unattainable. The gold dust from this locality has the unenviable notoriety of being of a lower grade of fineness than that from any other gulch in the Territory, coining from $12 to $14 per ounce, while the average of the other gulches runs from $16 50 up to $20 40 per ounce. The latter yield is producible only from choice and clean dust from high lands. This gulch and Silver Bow head in the same summit, and very nearly opposite to one another, the former being on the eastern and the latter on the western slope, and, curiously enough, the one produces the richest and the other the poorest gulch gold of Montana.

A few miles west of Silver Bow we find German gulch, tributary to Deer Lodge; it is some 15 miles long, and was discovered in 1864 by a party of Germans, who are believed to have been more than ordinarily successful.

The placer deposits of Montana have been worked with the same contrivances for saving gold as were used in California: the primitive rocker and the long-tom have given place to the improved strings of sluice boxes, and, where the ground permitted a sufficiency of fall. bed-rock flumes and hydraulics have lent their assistance to facilitate the extraction of the gold. Where the bed rock lay deep, and where the pay stratum was covered up to a considerable depth, the auriferous gravel was obtained by sinking shafts, drifting out and raising it to the surface by bucket and windlass.

In a country so widely covered with drift, many very rich deposits have, beyond question, been overlooked, owing to the great body of barren matter overlying them. This supposition is rendered the more probable when we reflect upon the small number of deep placers or cement diggings yet brought to light.

Assuming as true the usually accepted theory of the formation of placer deposits, viz., the disintegration of some pre-existing series of quartz veins, either by flowing waters or by the beating against them of the waves of some inland sea, and we cannot fail to accept the belief that placers richer and more extensive than any heretofore discovered yet await, under great hills of gravel, some fortunate prospector.

GOLD PRODUCT OF MONTANA.—We must premise any estimates by the statement of the peculiar difficulties of arriving at any conclusion susceptible of a demonstration. In the first place local interests and territorial pride combine with a mistaken estimate of the value of placer deposits to enlarge the returns of bullion. The surface washings ought not to be regarded other than in the light of an advertisement for a district; ephemeral producers of wealth, they leave nothing behind them but desolation, and unless supplemented by other sources of revenue, give rise to a fictitious prosperity, to be followed by a period of depression and stagnation. The hiatus between profitable placers and remunerative quartz mines is now apparent here in Montana. Some little time is requisite to educate the community, by hard experience, to a realization of the radical difference between surface washings and deep vein mining. The placers yield up their treasures with a comparatively trifling outlay of time and capital. The quartz veins, on the contrary, forming the basis for permanent undertakings and returns of profits through a long series of years, cannot be made immediately productive, except through fortuitous concurrence of favorable circumstances. Patience, foresight, and the exercise of a true economy, seldom fail to prevent great losses, and in most cases return an enormous profit.

The proportion of bullion produced by the vein mines has not, as yet, amounted to any considerable percentage of the gross yield, and hence does not call for a separate estimate. The year 1868, however, will doubtless demand from this source a more detailed consideration.

Another difficulty in the way of a precise statement of gold product is due to the fact that large quantities of dust can be, and doubtless have been removed northwardly into the British possessions of which no record is possible. Again, the distance of land transportation to Fort Benton, the head of navigation on the Missouri, is so trifling that merchants and miners act as their own transportation agents, and hence the precise amount carried away by them can never be ascertained. Montana's bullion account, at least until 1865, was largely credited to Washington, Idaho, or Colorado, and hence the tables as reported by the United States mints do not represent her true yield.

I am indebted to the United States revenue collector for the following figures, which form, in my judgment, a more reliable series of estimate for Montana than have ever been given to the public.

The product of 1862 may be set down at $600,000, and was due almost solely to the placers at Bannock. The great body of the miners were then very poor; no considerable stocks of goods were at hand to tempt purchasers, so that but a small proportion of the yield came into the possession of traders, whose shipments could be determined to a degree of reasonable exactness. In the absence of banks or any safe place of deposit the miners were accustomed to "cache" their earnings, and to await a favorable opportunity for exporting the gold from the country.

The product of the following year was largely increased by the discovery and partial opening of the mines of Alder gulch, and may safely be estimated to have reached a total of $8,000,000.

In 1864, Alder gulch was fully developed, and with Bannock and the other districts of the Territory, the amount produced reached some $16,000,000.

The year 1865 was the gala year of Montana, the rich network of gulches centring about Helena, the famous Confederate gulch across the Missouri, and the diggings near Blackfoot combined to swell the product to at least $18,000,000.

In the year 1866 the placers began so show symptoms of exhaustion; more extended workings were necessary. Great flumes and ditches were built, and hydraulics were undertaken to wash localities unworkable without the aid of capital, and by nature unsupplied with water. As a result we may estimate for that year a production of about $17,500,000.

The amount yielded by the present season, 1867, now nearly closed, has been very materially less than that of the past year, and a liberal estimate would not set the figure higher than $12,000,000. Tabulating the above figures, we have the following:

Gold product of Montana.

In 1862 a yield of	$600,000
In 1863 a yield of	8,000,000
In 1864 a yield of	16,000,000
In 1865 a yield of	18,000,000
In 1866 a yield of	17,500,000
In 1867 a yield of	12,000,000
Total for six years	72,100,000

As corroborative of the reasonableness of the above estimates, we may present the following conclusions derived from a multiplication of the total average population by the average cost of living.

As already stated, the population of the Territory during the three years 1864, 1865, and 1866 remained very nearly uniform, numbering from 21,000 to 24,000 souls. If now we place the average at 22,500, and assume that the great mass of the community were at the close of this period no better off pecuniarily than before; that is, that the placers have furnished a bare subsistence for the people and no more, and further, rating the average cost of living as low as $750 per annum for each individual, we have a total of $16,875,000 average amount of product of the placers for three years. Comparing this result with the average of the estimates of Mr. Langford and we find between them a remarkable coincidence and striking corroboration.

LODE MINING.—In treating of the distribution of the various metals and minerals reference was incidentally made to the districts containing quartz lodes. These have been found almost universally at the heads of the gulches or within a short distance of all localities heretofore noted as prolific centres of placer deposits. In addition, we have a number of districts unconnected with the gulch mines and productive of smelting or amalgamating ores, some of which are amongst those of greatest promise in the Territory.

It is as yet premature to speak of any extraordinary developments. This is owing to two causes, first, the youth of the Territory, and secondly, the peculiarity of the local laws. In this connection we may compare the laws and customs of the mid-continental territories with those of the Pacific coast. The latter are imbued with the spirit of the Mexican "Ordenanza de Mineria," in many respects the most perfect mining code ever invented, while the former are almost entirely a home production and are founded upon a totally different conception of mines and mining. The animus of the one implies that all miners are a priori valueless until the contrary be proven; that of the other presupposes precisely the reverse. The one encourages reasonably large holdings so that the ore zone on the vein diminishing or disappearing at one point may be sought for at another without incurring anew the outlay for shaft, hoisting works, pumps, &c., in a word, the expense of the complete paraphernalia of a working shaft; the other, with very small holdings and aggregated ownerships, complicates unnecessarily and unreasonably the risks attending most mining adventures.

The law of January 17, 1865, placing mining claims on the same footing as real estate, has resulted disadvantageously to the community, and has conferred upon the individual no other gain than the doubtful satisfaction of a clear title to what may or may not prove of value. No system of mining regulation can be beneficial which encourages the holding of quartz veins without even the pretence of developing them. Small holdings are commendable in the youth of the interest provided they are worked; otherwise they are a positive injury, and a drag on the wheels of development.

On the other hand, no legislation can meet with popular approval, nor indeed merits an instant's consideration, which does not include some plan for recognizing the services of the prospector. Generally poor, they incur every risk and privation to discover the location of the ore-bearing veins. Such men deserve at the hands of a just and parental government a treatment commensurate with their services. The rewards of mining adventures are not so numerous nor so equally distributed as to justify any legislation tending to cripple the miner or to diminish prospecting.

Too little legislation is far preferable to too much, and until the present congressional law be tried by the touchstone of practical experience, any further emendations or additions thereto are premature and pernicious. The leverage possessed by capital will, of itself, exert a sufficient power against the prospector, without the additional impetus of hostile legislation. The happy mean is to be sought, which, while it furthers prospecting and encourages development, does not bear too harshly upon the miner, and while it recognizes the merits of the *bona fide* claim-holder, does not screen the mere speculator.

It may be objected that many companies formed at a distance from Montana are possessed of many thousands of feet of quartz claims; this may readily be admitted, and still they bear the seeds of their own ruin, for the simple reason that they hold too many feet, too w'dely separated to be able properly to open any portion of them; and moreover should the company's enterprise disclose a valuable body of ore, they find themselves in possession of a contiguous stretch of vein too small to more than meet the outlays, when a larger ownership would have insured a brilliant profit. They find it further to be impossible to purchase the adjoining claims, whose value alone is due to their own labors.

These considerations will serve to account for the comparatively trifling development of the quartz interests of the Territory. Unlike the placers, winter offers not the least obstacle to a profitable exploration of the vein mines; the severity of the season rendering work in the open air difficult, if not impossible, redounds only to the interest of the quartz claims. Labor having no other field of employment is then abundant and cheap, and while the surface is wrapped in a mantle of snow and ice, the miner, under ground and unexposed to the elements, pursues his labors in an equitable and agreeable temperature.

Many of the best mines of the world are in countries visited with winters of far greater severity than those of Montana. The explorations are never retarded from this cause, and except as a source of physical inconvenience the severity of the weather is a matter of very trifling moment.

As the fairest exponents of the mining interests of Montana, we may select the following examples. Amongst the furthest developed and longest worked gold leads, we may instance the Oro Cache, near Virginia City, and the Owyhee or Whitlatch Union, near Helena City. As an example of the results of smelting, we have the case of the furnaces at Argenta, near Bannock; and lastly the veins west of the range in Flint creek and vicinity, which have recently been a point of considerable attraction from the promise of an abundance of silver ores suitable for amalgamation.

It will be impossible particularly to describe all or even any considerable proportion of the prospectively valuable vein mines of the Territory, whose future developments may change their present relative pre-eminence. In lieu thereof, I have selected such mines, works, &c., as, in my judgment, best exemplify the present status of the permanent mining interests of the Territory.

The Oro Cache lead is situated in the Summit district of Alder gulch, south of Virginia City. It was discovered as early as 1864, and work was begun thereon December 1 of the same year. The vein near the surface had a width of two feet, which gradually increased as the shaft was extended downwards. The average width is about 30 inches.

The surface ores, consisting of decomposed quartz, yielded from $75 to $100 currency per ton, while the average working yield of the clean ore has been up to the present time about $50 currency per ton.

A shaft 120 feet in depth has been sunk by the Montana Gold and Silver Mining Company on the second claim, of 200 feet, southwest of the point of discovery, and ore has been extracted yielding $50 currency per ton. The same company amalgamate the ores in pans 4 feet 10 inches in diameter, in which revolve two wheels, weighing two tons each. This method is said to be very effective in the reduction of the gold-bearing sulphurets. In the same district we find quite a number of promising quartz lodes, and four mill in or near Summit City.

The Whitlatch Union, sometimes called Owyhee lead, is situated south of Helena City, and on the divide between Oro Fino and Grizzly gulches. The lead was discovered during the winter of 1864, and work was begun in the succeeding spring. As this lode, up to the present time, has yielded a greater amount of bullion than any other in the Territory, it cannot be considered invidious to bestow upon it more than passing mention and description. This vein has given employment to two proprietary and two custom mills. Near the developed portion of the lead there has sprung up a flourishing mining town, known as Unionville or Rosevelt, the former appellation meeting with the more general acceptance. The country rock is granite, the micaceous component of which appears in the form of black scales. Near the surface the vein was broken in many places, running flat, and very irregularly. At the lowest points reached by the National Mining and Exploring Company of New York and the Whitlatch Union Mining Company of Helena, the vein, carrying a species of quartz differing somewhat from that near the surface, seems to have taken its true dip and direction. The width of the vein is variable from 20 inches to 5 or 6 feet, and at times widening out much further. The yield of the properly-cleaned rock averages between $50 and $60 per ton. The mean yield of the entire vein mass, has, however, run as high as $25 to $30 per ton.

The custom mills have taken the ore from the dump, and have crushed and amalgamated the same, according to the contracts, either for one-half the gross product in one mill or for $11 per ton in another. Captain W. W. De Lacy, who has made the survey of the lead, in accordance with the provisions of the congressional mining law, gives the direction of the vein south 84° 24' east. Adjoining one another on the lead are four different ownerships, viz: the Whitlatch Union Mining Company, the I. X. L. Mining Company, the National Mining and Exploring Company, and the Philadelphia Enterprise Company; of which the first is the only company possessing a contiguous holding of 500 feet.

ARGENTA SMELTING WORKS.—These works were constructed by the St Louis and Montana Mining Company, under the direction and personal supervision of Aug. Steitz, mining engineer, who unfortunately fell seriously ill very soon after their completion. They consist of one German double-cupola furnace, which is used for smelting the ore with appropriate fluxes, after it has been subjected to a calcination as thorough as possible in heaps or open hearths ; also a large German cupelling furnace, capable of holding at once a charge of five tons of rich lead, and so constructed as to admit of after charges to the total amount of 10 or more tons. The weight of the charge must be regulated according to the percentage of silver contained in the lead. Two fans, cased in wooden housings, and driven by a small steam engine, furnish a supply of air for the blast of the cupola and cupellation hearth. Each of these fans is about four feet in diameter; either of which, alone, is amply sufficient, but two have been constructed, to guard against the accidental breaking of the one or the other. The capacity of the furnace is, according to the ore, from two to five tons per day of 24 hours. The ores smelted, chiefly from the Legal-Tender lode, consist of carbonates and oxides of lead, and sulphurets of lead, or galenas.

The rich lead is tapped into an exterior basin as often as a sufficient quantity has been reduced from the ore to fill the furnace to the level of the fore-hearth, and has contained from $200 to $750 per ton—the last amount having been produced from a few tons of choice ore smelted under my direction in June last.

Besides the Argenta furnaces, we have near Bannock a lead furnace and cupellation hearth, recently constructed, for reducing the ores from the Huron district ; also, a second small furnace on the road between Argenta and Bannock. Further, there has been in operation, near Butte City, Deer Lodge county, a small furnace to test the copper-bearing ores of that vicinity. There is now building, and will shortly be in operation, an American hearth to smelt the ores of the Gregory lode, situated near Jefferson City, in the county of Edgerton. And lastly, the quartz mines of Flint Creek district. These leads are situated in Deer Lodge county, west of the main range, on an arm of Flint creek, 25 miles from its point of junction with the Hell Gate river.

In the vicinity of the mines there has sprung up quite an extensive town, called Phillipsburg. The district was discovered in December, 1864, by a prospector named Horton, while on a hunting excursion. Locations were made by him in the following May, and the district has received the name of the discoverer. Little was done until the present year, when a St. Louis company began the erection of a mill, with the appliances for amalgamating silver ores, ordered specially from California The locality, thus called prominently into notice, has been covered with a perfect forest of stakes, and every projecting rock has been located and recorded as a quartz lead. No bullion has been as yet produced other than a few small ingots of silver, the yield of an arrastra. The ores are generally of such a character as permit of reduction by amalgamation. Several of the principal lodes will, it is believed, return very large amounts of silver bullion.

COPPER.—Beside the small amount of copper regulus and black copper yielded by the experimental smelting furnace near Butte City, a considerable shipment of copper ores has been made from the mines at the head of the Muscleshell river. These properties, owned by capitalists of St. Louis, carry carbonates, oxides and silicates of copper, that is, the accustomed surface ores, while at greater depths will be found the usual yellow sulphurets. In this connection it may be permissible to state that a postal route has been established from Helena to St. Paul, Minnesota, along the Muscleshell river and past these mines. Efforts are now making to divert the carriage of freight from Fort Benton to a point at the mouth of this river. Steamers can reach the latter point so long as the river is not impeded by ice, while the former is accessible only during the time of the continuance of the increment from the melting snows. It is claimed that, though 60 miles longer, the route is better, and it certainly cuts off some 400 miles of the worst portion of the river navigation, and that, too, through a region almost totally destitute of timber.

Should these mines prove of value, this route would offer for the copper ores a cheap and expeditious means of transport to a market.

COAL.—Montana contains within her limits a large extent of valuable coal deposits. This "portable climate of civilization" is of the bituminous variety, and is referable to the cretaceous or tertiary age. This fact serves to corroborate the truth of the enunciation of Professor Whitney, of California, that the widest deposition of carbonaceous matters took place subsequently to the period heretofore denominated by geologists the coal period par excellence. The statements of Dr. Newberry in regard to the coal fields of China ; the age of the beds in California and Nevada; the discoveries of Aug. Rémond in Chili during the past year, and the localities examined by this gentleman and myself in the State of Sonora, Mexico, in the summer of 1864, all tend, in like manner, to a complete confirmation of that theory.

Of the many localities where traces of coal are to be found, and where beyond a doubt profitable beds may be met with, but one has been worked to any considerable extent, viz: on the Missouri river, some 110 miles below Fort Benton.

During the past winter several miners undertook to explore the coal seams with a view of supplying the steamers navigating the river. Having been tried under the boilers of several vessels it was reported to have been efficacious in some instances and worthless in others. The unfavorable opinion was perhaps owing to an imperfect separation of the shale from the coal, or because of the nonadaptation of the grate bars to the new fuel. Precisely similar results followed the preliminary trials of the coals from the Mount Diablo mines of the State of California. A larger experience has, however, approved their usefulness, until at present they form the sole fuel of hundreds of stationary engines, and are likewise used beneath the boilers of all the steamers plying upon the inland waters of the State. An excavation of some extent has likewise been made on a coal seam situated on Grasshopper creek, near Bannock.

COSTS OF MINING, MILLING, AND SMELTING.—It is impossible, from any considerable number of actual returns, to give the exact average of the costs of raising and reducing the ores of the Territory. A very general apathy in regard to the importance of publishing these data seems to possess the directors and managers of the mining properties of Montana, and but few responses have been received in answer to my printed circular soliciting these particulars in detail. Hence I shall be obliged to make estimates founded upon my own observations and the limited number of returns in my possession.

The prices of labor in Montana range from $5 to $10 currency per day. Wood costs, according to circumstances, from $3 to $10 currency per cord delivered, and generally $2 50 currency per cord cut and piled at the place of felling. Charcoal ranges from 33 cents currency to 40 cents in gold per bushel.

The lowest cost of raising the ore which has come under my observation must be credited to the Philadelphia Enterprise Company, working upon a portion of the Whitlatch Union lead, near Helena. The entire outlay debited to the raising of 1,300 tons was $3 36 currency per ton. I take these figures from the accounts of the superintendent, kindly submitted to my inspection. Again, we have the estimate of the agent of the Montana Gold and Silver Mining Company of Pennsylvania with regard to mining and delivering the ore from the U. S. Grant, a wide lode in Summit district, near Virginia City. By means of the tunnel, now nearly completed, the ore, should the promises of the surface be realized at that depth, may be mined and delivered at $4 currency per ton. In this connection it may be stated that all veins so situated as to be able to be worked by tunnel and tramway, can furnish ore at a very much smaller cost than such as require the use of shafts and hoisting apparatus. The necessity for pumping large amounts of water—a very material item of expense in deep mines—need not yet be taken into consideration regarding the mines of Montana. A reasonably wide vein under ordinary circumstances ought to be mined and laid upon the surface at a cost of from $5 to $8 per ton.

MILLING.—The Turnley and Hendrie mills, south of Helena, have crushed large amounts of gold quartz from the Whitlatch Union and Park lodes at from $11 to $12 per ton.

It is but reasonable to suppose that the custom mills have been able, at these figures, to return a profit; hence, under ordinarily favoring circumstances and judicious management, $15 per ton will cover all expense and yield a considerable profit; while a *working yield* of $20 to $25 in free gold will return cent per cent. on the requisite outlays.

SMELTING.—We have but one example of this method of reduction on a large scale, viz: the works of the St. Louis Company, at Argenta, Beaverhead county. It would be doing injustice to what may yet prove an important interest to assert that argentiferous galenas cannot be profitably reduced in Montana. It is but proper to enumerate the difficulties in the way of inaugurating new methods in a new country. Skilled smelters are almost if not quite unattainable; and such as offer themselves demand and receive very high rates of compensation. Charcoal is expensive, and it has not yet been proven whether the coals of the country are suitable for smelting purposes or not; and if so, whether they are to be found sufficiently near to the districts producing galenas and copper ores, which can only be reduced by smelting. Thus much, however, is certain—the amalgamation is more expeditious and far cheaper; the one performs most of the labor by machinery, that is, is thoroughly in consonance with the spirit and genius of the people; the other necessitates repeated handlings and much manual labor, and hence its greater expensiveness. As the country becomes better settled, with lower rates of wages and diminished cost of food and materials, smelting may possibly compete with the amalgamation. While fully acknowledging the statements of its advocates in claiming a more thorough extraction of the precious metals, candor compels an assent to its greater costliness. Ores containing less than $100 per ton cannot, in my judgment, be at present smelted with a profit. With water power to drive the mechanism for furnishing a blast—be it bellows, fans, or cylinders—and with a sufficiency of suitable ores and abundant timber near to the works, smelting may be done at the present time at a cost of $60 to $80 per ton.

OTHER RESOURCES.—The future prosperity of Montana is by no means dependent upon the precious metals alone. She has other and prolific sources of wealth, among which we may mention the following, now awaiting exploration and development:

Large masses of fire clay occur in the coal measures, which cannot fail to be of permanent usefulness should smelting ores be found in sufficient abundance. Iron ores and plumbago are known to exist.

Moss agates are found in several localities, some of which show most curious and beautiful markings. Very fine specimens of the common garnet occur in a vein-like dike near Summit City, near Virginia. True sapphires and one or two diamonds are said to have been found on El Dorado bar, near the Missouri river.

Argilaceous sandstones and marbles fit for building purposes are of quite common occurrence. Near the mouth of the Beaver Head cañon is already established a manufactory of grindstones.

CONCLUSION.—Such, briefly sketched, is the present status of the mineral industries of the Territory of Montana. The developments already made are, considering the youth of the interest, most satisfactory, and as furnishing an earnest for the future cannot but prove encouraging to every promoter of legitimate enterprise.

A better appreciation of the rewards and risks of mining undertakings cannot fail to advance the well-being of the industry, at the same time that it militates against purely speculative adventures.

That the profits to be derived from mines, selected with judgment and under an honorable and experienced superintendence, are not to be considered in the light of vague possibilities, which can neither be estimated nor foreseen, let us compare the returns derived from railways, canals, water-works, gas, dock and land companies, with those derived from mines—all held in the city of London.* It was found that the yield from the former species of investments equalled 3¼ per cent. on the average selling price, while that from the latter, based upon the 350 mines in the mining share list, including lead, copper, and tin, made an annual dividend of 13¼ per cent. If, now, the mining adventures of English capitalists are, on the average, more than three times as productive as any of the aforementioned investments, while those in the hands of American owners have, though far richer, so often failed to cover even the ordinary running expenses—if this be the case, it behooves one to investigate the causes of and to seek the remedy for so marked a difference.

The chief source of this most deplorable result lies in the supposed necessity of mystery in regard to costs, yields, &c. Until mine and mill owners can be made to understand the usefulness to themselves of comparative data as well as the benefit to the interest at large, it will be hopeless to expect that the great body of the community will be able to discriminate between reasonable and unreasonable undertakings. All persons engaged in mining, as a legitimate pursuit, should contribute to dispel this ignorance, for the reason that every dollar lavished on mere speculation is not only so much withdrawn from actual production, but also reacts unfavorably on further investments.

Montana has, up to the present time, been comparatively free from purely speculative schemes.

The main obstacle in the way of the success of those mines which are held by non-resident owners has been, as already stated, the diffusion of their energies over too wide a field and the injudicious selection of small segregated holdings.

These errors of the past may be easily avoided in the future, and companies using proper precautions in selecting and due diligence in opening their mines before purchasing or erecting machinery of any kind, can hardly fail to meet with most remunerative returns.

Montana need not blush to compare her treasures of the precious and useful minerals with those of any other section. She has within her limits as great a variety of metalliferous veins as any single State or Territory. Veins bearing free gold and amalgable silver ores are those immediately available, while argentiferous galenas, copper ores, and coals will, at some future day, afford an exhaustless field for permanent and profitable investment, particularly when the Northern Pacific railroad shall have facilitated communication and diminished the outlays for freight

---

SECTION IV.

GOLD AND COAL MINES OF NOVA SCOTIA.

HALIFAX, NOVA SCOTIA, *January* 1, 1868.

SIR: I beg leave to offer the following statements and observations relative to the mines and mineral resources of Nova Scotia, in the hope that they may be considered worth being embodied in the report which, I have understood, you are preparing upon the mineral resources of the United States and British provinces east of the Rocky mountains.

Mines are officially classified in Nova Scotia as "gold mines" and "mines other than gold." I shall observe the same classification in treating of them and the minerals which they develop. In the course of the following remarks I trust that, to relieve myself from again going over ground which I have previously trodden—some of it several times—I may be pardoned for occasionally making extracts from former papers of mine upon the same subject, and from official reports prepared by me, during the past four years, as gold commissioner and chief commissioner of mines. First, then, as to gold mines.

Gold-bearing, geological formations, form a large portion of the surface of Nova Scotia. To indicate their character and extent I will make an extract, brief, indeed, but sufficient, I trust, for our present purpose, from a paper prepared and read by me before the "Nova Scotia Institute of National Science," on the 6th of February, 1866:

The outlines of the well-marked geological district which comprises the gold fields of Nova Scotia, are already pretty generally known. I will only briefly state that they mainly consist of two distinct districts of different geological ages. We have upon the Atlantic coast the Lower Silurian rocks, forming a band which extends the whole length of the Nova Scotian peninsula. This district is not less than 50 miles in width at its western extremity, gradually narrowing as it proceeds eastward, and finally coming almost to a point at Cape Canso. The other district, the Devonian and Upper Silurian, forms several comparatively lofty and isolated ridges. One of these extends from Digby county, along the south side of the Annapolis valley, to the vicinity of Windsor. Another commences at Cape Chiegnecto, forms the Cobequid hills, and, with a slight divergence from its original course, proceeds eastward to the Strait of Canso, throwing off spurs northeastward to the Gulf of St. Lawrence, and southwestward on both sides of the Stewiacke river. In the island of Cape Breton, nearly the whole of Victoria county, a large portion of Inverness, and several detached eminences in Cape Breton and Richmond counties, belong to the same formation. Among the gold-bearing formations of this province I might also include the Trap ridges, considerable as to extent, for auriferous quartz has been discovered and to some slight extent mined in the Trappean headlands of Partridge island and Cape D'Or; but I will leave this geological district out of further consideration. The extent of the two larger districts which I have indicated, comprises, in the aggregate, a large proportion of the surface of Nova Scotia. I would roughly estimate the area of the Lower Silurian district at 7,000 square miles, and of the several tracts of the more recent formation at 3,000, in all 10,000 square miles. The whole area of the province amounts to about 18,600 square miles. It must not be assumed that this large area is throughout auriferous. I will observe, parenthetically, that, judging from what is already known. there is every reason to believe that future explorations will prove the greater part of this area to be rich in metalliferous deposits of some kind.

As to gold I will begin with the Devonian district. The several ridges of highlands which come under this denomination have, as yet, been but little explored for gold; nor is it probable that they will be, to any great extent, for some time to come. These hills are, for the most part, in the interior of the country. Their rocks are rarely exposed, being covered with a pretty deep soil from which has arisen a heavy growth of timber. Gold has been found in the alluvium brought down by many streams which take their rise in these hills. It has seldom been discovered, as yet, in quartz *in situ*, but, for the reasons just referred to, quartz *in situ* has seldom been seen in this geological district. In Wagamatkook, which is a proclaimed gold district, about the head waters of the river of the same name, in Victoria county, quartz has been mined to some small extent. The little done here in this way did not afford as good promise of profit as has been met with in quartz mining elsewhere in the province, but it cannot be considered a fair test of the productiveness of the district. Most of the gold obtained at Wagamatkook has been taken from the beds of streams which flow down from the hills, and the quantity thus procured indicates the presence of numerous auriferous quartz veins in the vicinity. Gold has been discovered in the sands of nearly all, if not all, the streams of Victoria and Inverness, which take their rise in these metamorphic hills. It has also been found in the same formation at Cape Porcupine, near the head waters of the Musquodoboit and the Stewiacke, and, I believe, at Five Islands and elsewhere, so that gold may be sought for, with not unreasonable expectations of success, in any part of this geological district.

We have more reliable data as to the auriferous character of the better known Lower Silurian coast band. We know that in the Lower Silurian district there are found bands of quartzite seemingly nearly parallel with each other, alternating with various slates, extending in a general easterly and westerly direction. These bands are intersected by various masses of granite, in some places extending quite across the whole formation, but more frequently forming detached masses, protruding through, and surrounded by, the stratified rocks just named. In this quartzite, and, in a less degree, in some of the slates, we find numerous veins of quartz; and these veins, especially those of the quartzite, we find to be auriferous. Of the number of the quartzite bands, and of the latitudinal extent of each, little is yet known. From a general acquaintance with the country, and not from actual survey, I am inclined to the belief that, in the aggregate, they form the largest portion of the width, superficially, of this metamorphic district skirting the Atlantic.

Longitudinally this quartzite, with its auriferous quartz veins, can, except when interruptions are caused by the granite dikes already mentioned, be traced the whole length of the Nova Scotia peninsula. Gold has been taken from quartz veins at Yarmouth and on the shore of Chedabucto bay, and, I might add, at every intermediate point where diligent search has been made for it in the proper formation. The quantity of quartz embraced in this great length and breadth of quartzite veinstone must be something enormous. I speak of it in comparison with the bulk of the enclosing rock. Of course we have no sufficient data from which to estimate this quantity. The opinion I have just hazarded is based upon observations of the cross cuttings in the rock yet made in the few localities of this province where gold mining is yet carried on, and these openings have in many, I believe I might say in most instances, been made at mere hap-hazard. On one occasion I myself removed carefully the drift, so as to expose a cross section of the surface merely of the bed-rock, for a distance of about 160 feet. Within that distance I discovered over 30 quartz veins ranging from an inch to 15 inches in thickness. The whole number of veins would average not less than six inches, or say 15 feet in all, thickness of quartz in 160 feet of enclosing rock, the dip being here nearly vertical. In another instance, after counting and measuring the quartz veins exposed within a distance of 250 feet, I estimated their aggregate thickness at 25 feet; and yet, as within a part of the distance of 250 feet there was no exposure of the bed-rock, the actual thickness of this quartz may have been considerably greater than what I have stated. In both of these cases the quartz veins exposed, or the greater number of them, were known to be auriferous from examination made at the several spots where laid bare. In other localities quartz veins of 5, 10, and even up to 30 feet in thickness, are found, but I will not multiply instances. Those which I have specified do not, I think, exhibit a much greater thickness of quartz in proportion to that of the enclosing rock than will be found generally throughout these quartzite bands.

Such is, in brief, a description of the auriferous districts of Nova Scotia. As to the most important of these, economically speaking, viz : the Lower Silurian, the operations being carried on throughout its whole extent are almost exclusively those of quartz mining. Owing to the conformation of the country, no part of this district being estimated to attain a greater elevation than 500 feet above sea level, and the whole of it lying in immediate propinquity to the sea, the deposits of auriferous diluvium and alluvium to be found in the more mountainous and inland gold-fields west of the Rocky mountains, and in Australia and elsewhere, are few in Nova Scotia, and of very limited extent. Following what seems to have been the course of the current which has produced a partial denudation of the rocks of the Atlantic coast band, the disintegrated rock thus set free has been swept into the Atlantic. Accordingly we find that at most points along that coast, where anything like a thorough examination is practicable, the sands of the shore contain a greater or less proportion of gold. The same remark applies to Sable island, off the eastern coast of Nova Scotia. This island consists altogether of sand into the composition of which gold enters to such an extent that it is believed, by those who have experimented in the matter, that gold washing on a large scale could here be carried on at a handsome profit.

I have already mentioned that this Lower Silurian district embraces a number of quartzite bands maintaining an easterly and westerly course. It must be added that each of these quartzite bands represents a distinct line of upheaval, and has its anticlinal axis. Consequently a section crossing the whole district at right angles with the coast line, would represent a series of undulations of strata. The quartz veins, or, more properly speaking, beds, have generally the same strike and dip as the strata enclosing them. "Cross leads," as they are called by the miners, or veins cutting the strata transversely, are of not unfrequent occurrence; but, as a rule, they are found to be comparatively unproductive in gold. I shall presently have to notice some exceptions to this.

The conditions under which gold is found in these quartz lodes are extremely varied. In many instances, probably in a majority of cases yet observed, the lode itself has a casing of dark-blue clay slate, or talcose slate, on one side, or both, but more frequently the former. In other cases nothing intervenes between the quartz vein and the enclosing quartzite rock. In some instances the lode consists more of slate than of quartz; and, frequently, both in this case and in that of the slaty casing just mentioned, the slate itself is found to be as profusely impregnated with gold as even the quartz is. Sometimes a quartz lead is of a snowy whiteness throughout, interspersed with gold of perfect purity unassociated with any other mineral; but more frequently these lodes are highly mineralized, mispickel or arsenical pyrites, zinc blende, and oxides of iron, being the prevalent associated minerals, the first named pre-eminently so. Throughout the Nova Scotia mines the gold, as taken from its matrix, is, when compared with the immediate product of other mines in the world, of unsurpassed if not unsurpassable purity. Owing in part to this fact the treating of auriferous ores to extract the gold from them is beset with comparatively few difficulties in Nova Scotia.

The discovery of gold in Nova Scotia was a very remarkable incident; remarkable, not because gold was actually discovered, but because it was not discovered at a much earlier period in the political history of this country. This fact becomes particularly striking when we remember that gold was a special object of inquiry among the earlier European navigators who visited our shores: that Nova Scotia is the site of the oldest European settlement in America north of Florida; and that the auriferous rocks, composing so large a proportion of the surface of the whole country, crop out upon its surface, and are found to exhibit gold at the surface of the outcrop at almost innumerable localities. As to when and by whom it was first discovered there is a diversity of legends and some disputes. At all events, the first unmistakable discoveries, which the public felt bound to take notice of, are thus described in the gold commissioner's first annual report—that for 1862:

The earliest discovery of gold in the province, made known to the public, occurred during the summer of 1860, at a spot about 12 (it is less than 10) miles north from the head of Tangier harbor, on the northeast branch of the Tangier river. The discoverer, John Pulsifer, of Musquodoboit, was induced, from what he had heard of the gold-bearing quartz of California, to search for the same substance amongst the rocks on the upper waters of the Tangier river; and, while in company with some Indians whom he had hired, Mr. Pulsifer found several pieces of gold in quartz, in a brook at a place now known as the Moosland diggings, or, more frequently, Old Tangier, owing to this circumstance. This discovery being known a number of persons gathered to the spot from various parts of the province, during the summer and the succeeding autumn, for the purpose of prospecting.

In the month of October, of the same year, Peter Mason, a fisherman and landowner near the head of Tangier harbor, was passing through the woods about half a mile from his own residence and on his own land; he stooped to drink at a small brook, noticed a particle of shining yellow metal in a piece of quartz which was there very abundant, and having picked it up and examined it he concluded, from what he had heard of the discovery of gold up the river, that he also had found the precious metal. Upon this fact becoming known a number of the inhabitants in the vicinity of Tangier flocked to the locality and commenced a search for the supposed source from which the specimen had been derived.

The public attention was now fully aroused, and with the opening of the following spring, that of 1861, gold mining in a rude way was commenced at Tangier, for the regulation of which and the appropriation of land for mining purposes, the provincial government found it necessary to frame certain "orders in council." Explorations were also prosecuted with vigor both at Tangier and elsewhere in the coast band of metamorphic rocks. The consequence was that during the ensuing summer promising discoveries of gold were made at the Ovens, in Lunenburg county; Lawrencetown, Waverley, and Oldham, in Halifax county; Renfrew, in Hants county; Sherbrooke, Wine Harbor, and Isaac's Harbor, in Greysborough county, and elsewhere. These places still comprise the greater number of the, as yet known, most productive gold districts of the province. Of the others which have become particularly noted, Montagu, about six miles from Halifax, in the county of the same name, was discovered in the spring of 1863; Wagamatkook, in Victoria county, in the summer of the same year; and Uniacke, Hants county, in 1865.

As one of the best modes of illustrating the character and exhibiting the progress of gold mining in Nova Scotia, it may be well to give a few sentences to each of these districts, taking them separately. To begin at the most western, then, the Ovens are so called from the shapes of a succession of caverns which, by the action of the sea-waves, have been washed out from the face of a low cliff on the west side and near the mouth of Malegash bay. Gold was here first discovered among the sands along the shore beach, and in such quantity as to cause no small excitement at the outset. At first it was supposed that the auriferous sands were thrown up from the bed of the neighboring sea, for gold was found in increased quantity after every storm which drove the waves in shore. It was eventually learned that this result was produced by the action of the waves in sapping the face of the rock forming a cross section of an auriferous band of the shore itself. The washing of these sands was carried on with vigor for some time, but has, of late, been almost wholly abandoned. The process was found to be an expensive one, and the area over which it could be carried on very limited. The auriferous band of the shore itself at this place presents some characteristics seldom met with in the other gold districts of the province. The quartz veins, although numerous and rich, are comparatively thin, and the "cross leads"—true veins cutting the strata transversely—are the richest in gold, a fact seldom met with elsewhere in Nova Scotia.

The Ovens is one of the oldest known gold districts in Nova Scotia, and those who first invested money there seem to have entertained most extravagant expectations of the richness of the place. Their anticipations were not realized, and consequently, in the reaction which took place in the public mind, the place was unreasonably cried down. It is beyond doubt that gold mining can be carried on at the Ovens with fair profits.

Waverley is situated 10 miles distant from Halifax by the post road to Truro, and about 12 miles distant from the same place by railway. Thus far Waverley has produced a larger gross amount of gold than any other district in the province, a result which is in a large degree attributable to the favorable situation of the place, and the unwonted vigor with which mining operations have there been carried on by two or three of the most largely interested companies, for the average yield of gold per ton of quartz, over the whole district and for a period of six years, has been less at Waverley than at several other districts. The most effective rule to apply in order to ascertain, at least approximately, the profit derivable from a mine, or from a whole district, is to show the product of gold for each man engaged in and about mining. In 1863, the first year in which complete official returns were obtained, Waverley gave $258 40 per man for the year. This rate has gradually increased year by year, until, in 1865, it amounted to $395 87. There was a slight falling off during the ensuing years.

Lawrencetown is about 12 miles eastward of Halifax, between the great eastern shore road and the shore of the Atlantic itself, and is of easy access. Since 1861 mining has been carried on at this place with varying success, operations being wholly suspended at intervals. It was not until the latter part of 1866 that the real value of this gold field came to be appreciated. Since then a large portion of the district has fallen into new hands; some very rich lodes have been struck, and mining has been prosecuted with considerable vigor.

Montagu, six miles eastward of Halifax, and of easy access by post road, has not been distinguished by the same activity which has characterized operations in some other districts. Nevertheless the ground is favorably situated for mining; and the monthly and yearly returns of its gold product are rather remarkable for the slight degree of fluctuation they exhibit. These for the year ending 30th of September last showed a product of $406 60 per man.

I may here observe that since 1864 the 30th September has been held as the termination of the fiscal year in Nova Scotia. Consequently when, hereafter, I speak of any returns for either of the years 1865, 1866 or 1867, I allude to the twelvemonth ending with the 30th September of the year in question.

That part of *Oldham* district in which the principal mining operations have heretofore been carried on is about three miles eastward of Enfield railway station, which station is 27 miles distant by rail from Halifax. Owing to causes which are attributable less to the nature of the place than to the management of those who have invested there, mining has been less uniformly successful there than in some other localities. Oldham has the distinction of having shown a larger *maximum yield* of gold than any other district. At one time this amounted to 103 ounces, 14 dwts. per ton of quartz. In another respect it is almost singular, for a "cross vein" of quartz has here proved to be one of the most productive lodes in the district.

Renfrew is distant about seven miles westward from Enfield railway station, already mentioned. From 1862 to 1865, inclusive, mining was carried on in this district on no very extensive scale, but with fair and increasing profits, and a gradual extension of operations. In 1866, owing to an influx of additional mining capital, and the opening of a number of new lodes, a great stride in advance was made, and the aggregate gold product for that year was more than five times that of the last previous year. This prosperity has continued unabated to the present time, and in 1867 the Renfrew mines afforded $895 30 per man.

The centre of *Uniacke* mines is about three miles eastward of Mount Uniacke railway station, this station being 26 miles by the Windsor Branch railway from Halifax, and 22 from Windsor. Mining may be said to have really commenced in the early part of 1867, the first important discoveries of gold having been made there during the preceding year. The prospects throughout the district, so far as explorations have been extended, are very promising, and mining, where it has been carried on, has shown large returns. The operations of one company at Uniacke, for some months during the latter part of 1867, yielded at the rate of an ounce of gold per day per man, a larger average, I believe, than has been shown elsewhere in Nova Scotia.

Tangier is upon the Atlantic coast, 56 miles eastward from Halifax by post road, and about the same distance by water. This district, although an exceedingly rich one beyond all question, has been subject to great and frequent fluctuations, owing mainly, in the first instance, to the injudicious mining regulations adopted by the government when gold was first discovered there; and secondly, to the business complications of those into whose hands a large portion of the mining ground subsequently fell. This district is divided into two sections, known as blocks A and B, or Old Tangier and Tangier proper. The latter lies immediately upon the shore about the tide-waters of the safe and commodious havens of Tangier and Pope's harbor, and consequently possesses great facilities of access. Old Tangier, as already mentioned, is situated about nine miles back from the shore. Although this was the first spot where gold was mined in Nova Scotia, the operations carried on there are still upon a somewhat limited scale. This has been owing to the difficulties of access to the place. Latterly, however, a road has been opened through the wilderness, and mining has there been renewed with much spirit. The quartz lodes are numerous, continuous, and of even thickness, and yield a good average of gold. A large quantity of specimens of auriferous nuggety quartz taken from old Tangier during the latter part of 1867 exceed in richness and brilliancy anything of their kind previously found in Nova Scotia.

Sherbrooke gold district lies upon the west side of St. Mary's river. It is 150 miles from Halifax by the most direct land route, and about two-thirds of that distance by water. This district has been one of the largest producers of gold in Nova Scotia. It has also been, perhaps, one of the most uninterruptedly successful, a fact which, however, I am inclined to attribute less to the exceeding richness of the mines than to the skill and energy with which they have been worked. The profits of mining in Sherbrooke have continued to increase steadily year by year. This can scarcely be questioned when we find that the annual yield of gold has attained an average of $1,592 58 for every man employed.

Wine Harbor gold district is situate upon the harbor of the same name, four miles eastward of the mouth of St. Mary's river, already named. During the first four years of its mining history, this district kept pace with Sherbrooke as a gold producer—indeed, rather surpassed the latter place. Since then there has been something of a falling off in the product. This is mainly owing to the fact that latterly the parties most largely interested at Wine Harbor have engaged a large share of their joint efforts in works which are not immediately productive, but which are essential to an extension of mining operations. There seems to be no reason to doubt that the place will soon resume its former high position as a gold district.

Isaac's Harbor or *Stormont* district is advantageously situated upon one of the finest harbors upon the eastern coast, and is about 20 miles eastward of the mouth of St. Mary's river. This district has also been a large producer in proportion to the amount of effort that has there been put forth in mining; but enterprises of that class have never yet been entered into upon anything like a large scale. The possibilities of the place may be imagined from the fact that, taking the whole period since gold mining commenced in Nova Scotia, we find that the mines of Isaac's harbor have kept up the largest average yield of gold per ton of quartz.

The situation of *Wagamatkook* is comparatively remote from the centres of population, being in the wooded highlands of the interior of Victoria county. The difficulty of access to it has militated against its prosperity as a mining district. Another cause of its lack of prosperity is to be found in the fact that a large portion of its most promising ground remained for a long time in the hands of parties who did little or nothing to develop it. Indeed, little more can be said of Wagamatkook than that it affords very promising indications as a gold field; but that much may be alleged with perfect safety.

The progress of development of these mining districts, although not very rapid, has been continuous, steady, and increasingly satisfactory. The aggregate quantity of gold produced by them was, in 1862, 7,275 ounces; in 1863, 14,001 ounces, 14 pennyweights, 17 grains: in 1864, for nine months ending September 30, 14,565 ounces, 9 pennyweights, 8 grains; in 1865, for 12 months ending September 30, 24,867 ounces, 5 pennyweights, 22 grains; in 1866, 24,162 ounces, 4 pennyweights, 11 grains; in 1867, 27,583 ounces, 6 pennyweights, 9 grains.

In another respect, these results are more gratifying. There are no returns of the number of men engaged in mining in 1862; but in 1863 the total quantity of gold produced was equivalent to $296 to every man engaged in and about gold mining in Nova Scotia during the year. In 1864, this average had attained, for nine months only, $324 66 per man; in 1865, $664 80; in 1866, $669 41; and in 1867, $765 per man for the 12 months, equal to $2 44 per man per day. In all these calculations gold is estimated at $18 50 per ounce, which is less than its real value.

When the first of these averages was made known to the public, it was clearly shown that the mines of Nova Scotia in the aggregate yielded a larger average product per man engaged in mining than those of any other country, and this average has been nearly trebled in four years. In fact, although the above calculations do not necessarily prove it, the results produced from the various gold mines of Nova Scotia, taken separately, do not present those striking contrasts observable in every other gold-producing country. We seldom hear of such extraordinarily rich prizes as are, at times, met with elsewhere, but, on the other hand, a mine which is a total failure—which does not at least yield a moderate profit—is a very rare exception.

It will be seen that, with the exception of the last named, and even that may scarcely be considered an exception, all of the gold districts above briefly described are easily accessible, lying, as they do, immediately upon a coast abounding with superior harbors, or within a very few miles of the great interior thoroughfares of the province. They are so situate that they can be readily supplied with all the requisites of a mining district at a low rate of charge. When one considers this fact, together with that of the productive character of the mines themselves, he may naturally wonder at the paucity of the numbers engaged in mining, and of the consequent aggregate result of their operations. Doubtless, in the very propinquity of Nova Scotia to Great Britain, the Atlantic States, and the other Canadian provinces, the sources from which most great commercial enterprises emanate, and the facility with which reliable auriferous districts may be reached, become possessed, and profitably developed in Nova Scotia, may be found, in great measure, the solution of the problem thus suggested. There probably never was an adage more pregnant with truth than that embodied in the oft quoted poetical line:

'Tis distance lends enchantment to the view.

Even from Nova Scotia itself people sometimes go to Colorado, Columbia, California, Australia, or New Zealand, to mine gold, thus abandoning at least ten chances in their favor at home for one that they can pick up abroad.

Comparing the prospects with the results, as above set forth, it will be seen that gold mining is yet in its infancy in Nova Scotia. We may further infer that the discovery of localities in which gold mining can be carried on with profit has scarcely more than commenced. Among the places not already named where gold has been discovered, with good prospects of profitable mining, may be mentioned Cranberry Head, at the extreme western limit of the province, in Yarmouth county; Gold river, in Lunenburgh county; Boar's Back, near Gay's river, and Stewiacke, in Colchester; East river, Chizzelcook, Musquodoboit, Scraggy Lake, Killagg river, and elsewhere on the Sheet Harbor rivers and their branches, in Halifax county; and the shores of Chedabucto bay and Cape Porcupine, in Guysborough county. The existence of auriferous deposits in some of these places has been known for years; in others it is of recent discovery.

It may not be out of place, in this paper, to give a brief outline of the more important provisions of the law of Nova Scotia relating to gold mines. It must be premised that, whoever may be the owner of the land, gold mines in Nova Scotia belong, in the first instance, to the Crown. At least, this is practically the case as yet. There are portions of land in the province which have been granted without reserving to the Crown any minerals, but upon such unlimited grants no gold has yet been discovered. As a rule, out of all land granted in Nova Scotia there are reserved to the Crown all mines and deposits of gold, silver, lead, tin, iron, copper, and coal. All other mineral substances are conveyed with the soil.

The regulations improvised by the governor and council on the first discovery of gold in Nova Scotia, as also the first "gold field act" passed by the provincial legislature, were framed, as might naturally enough be supposed, with but a very imperfect knowledge of what was requisite to a gold mining community anywhere, still more of all that was peculiar in the Nova Scotian gold fields, and would most conduce to their development. Consequently they were hampered with many provisions which experience soon proved to be useless, but which bore heavily and vexatiously upon those who engaged in mining enterprises. There is little room to doubt that the check thus given to such enterprises at their very conception is, in its results, felt to some extent even yet. The law now in force, which, with its subsequent amendments, was framed by the writer of this paper, has been found to work satisfactorily to all parties concerned, although, of course, every year's additional experience suggests some further amendation.

According to the existing law, the intending miner, having determined upon the site of his future operations, it not being preoccupied by another, may, in the first instance, apply at the department of mines for either a "prospective license," or a lease. There is no limit to the extent of ground that he may apply for. To obtain a prospecting license he must pay at the rate of 50 cents per acre, and, where the ground applied for is not Crown land, must enter into a bond to reimburse the proprietor thereof for any damage that may be done to his land. This license holds good for three months, but is renewable for a further term of three months upon the prepayment of 25 cents per acre. This gives him the exclusive right to explore over the whole tract applied for, and select any part, or the whole of it, upon which to carry on mining operations.

Before entering upon any such mining operations, he must, whether he has previously held a prospecting license or not, apply for a lease of such unoccupied ground as he may have selected for his purpose. On making such application, he is required to pay at the rate of $2 for each area of 250 feet in length by 150 feet in breadth; and, also, when the ground applied for is private property, to make an arrangement with the owner of the soil for any damages the latter is likely to sustain. Thereupon he receives a lease for 21 years, reserving a royalty of two and one-half per cent. upon all the gold mined. The law further requires him to have labor performed annually at the rate of 100 days' work for every 250×150 feet leased by him; and to furnish quarterly, and swear to, a return showing, among other things, the amount of work and where performed, the quantity of quartz mined, the mill to which it was sent, and the quantity of gold obtained from it.

Any person is liable to a heavy fine who runs a quartz mill without a license. Before obtaining this license, for which there is no charge, he must give bonds with ample sureties for the performance of his duties as required by law. The licensed mill owner must every month make and swear to a return showing the quantity of quartz crushed, the mine whence it came, and the quantity of gold taken from it; and out of this gold he himself pays to the mines department the royalty reserved by law, receiving three per cent. out of that royalty commission for his trouble.

It will thus be seen that every pains has been taken to insure reliability in the statistical returns furnished from the Nova Scotian gold fields. A glance at this outline of the leading provisions of the law will convince the reader that, at least, there can be no exaggeration in the statistical statement above set forth, or in the tables appended to this paper. Doubtless some gold is smuggled away from the mines without paying royalty, and consequently never appears in the official returns. The amount which is thus eliminated from the auriferous products of the country cannot be estimated with anything approaching to accuracy.

The following yearly abstracts of the results of gold mining operations from 1863 to 1867, inclusive, shows the progress that has been made and the aggregate product, so far as official returns can show them:

Abstract of gold mining statistics—1863.

Districts.	Average men employed.	Crushing mills in dist.	Steam power.	Water power.	Quartz, sand, and gravel crushed.	Yield per ton.	Gold from alluvial mines.	Total yield of gold.	Maximum yield per ton.	Average annual yield portion engaged in mining.
					Tons Cwt. Lbs	Oz. Dwt. Gr	Oz. Dwt. Gr	Oz. Dwt. Gr.	Oz. Dwt. Gr	
Isaac's Harbor...	50	1	1	0	526 11 0	3 0 7	....	1,587 13 12	8 0 0	$587 30
Wine Harbor	124	4	3	1	3,644 10 0	1 0 10	....	3,718 2 19	66 0 0	555 00
Sherbrooke	100	5	4	1	3,454 1 68	19 0	28 0 0	3,304 14 12	12 0 0	611 49
Tangier.	120	6	3	3	655 9 40	15 2	....	494 8 21	4 0 0	76 20
Lawrencetown...	6	1	1	0	123 10 0	10 11	....	64 17 12	Unknown.	200 00
Montagu	124	0	0	0	139 18 0	2 16 2	....	366 14 16	5 9 8	55 50
Waverley	187	5	5	0	6,754 19 15	7 1	....	2,380 6 3	17 14 0	258 40
Oldham	83	8	5	3	1,025 16 33	1 4 6	....	1,223 3 21	43 13 6	272 60
Renfrew........:	68	4	2	2	574 17 0	1 7 7	....	785 7 7	6 6 0	203 90
Ovens	15	1	1	0	102 1 59	4 13 23	....	76 5 14	9 0 0	89 40
Total......	877	35	25	10	17,001 14 15	16 12	28 0 0	14,001 14 17	66 0 0	296 00

Abstract of gold mining statistics—1864.

Districts.	Average men employed.	Crushing mills employed, Sept. 30,'64.	Steam power.	Water power.	Quartz, sand, and gravel crushed.	Yield per ton.	Gold from alluvial mines.	Total yield of gold.	Maximum yield per ton.	Average yield for 9 months per man engaged in mining gold, $18 50 per oz.
					Tons. Cwt. Lbs	Oz. Dwt. Gr	Oz. Dwt. Gr	Oz. Dwt. Gr.	Oz. Dwt. Gr	
Stormont, Isaac's Harbor.	78	2	1	1	391 10 0	2 14 2½	....	1,049 4 21	8 10 0	$348 80
Wine Harbor	77	4	3	1	2,738 0 0	1 2 18	....	3,190 9 5	16 0 0	749 73
Sherbrooke	113	4	3	1	1,909 12 0	1 7 8	....	2,611 22 22	29 0 0	427 51
Tangier	51	6	3	3	468 17 0	15 11	....	363 2 0	2 7 20	131 67
Montagu.........	37	....	....	....	304 15 0	2 2 15	....	649 8 23	3 10 0	324 50
Waverley.........	279	6	5	1	6,979 14 0	12 17	....	4,491 3 0	20 0 0	297 80
Oldham.........	134	7	4	3	1,757 0 0	15 12	....	1,362 15 8	163 14 0	188 14
Renfrew	43	5	3	2	750 6 0	1 3 7	....	874 5 6	6 1 0	385 00
Other and unproclaimed districts.	19	1	1	....	17 0 0	6 1	38 11 3	43 13 19	....	42 54
	830	35	23	12	15,316 14 0	19 0	38 11 3	14,563 9 8	103 14 0 4 cwt.fr'm small lode.	324 66

Abstract of gold mining statistics—1865.

Districts.	Average men employed.	Crushing mills employed Sept. 30, '65.	Steam power.	Water power.	Quartz, sand, and gravel crushed.	Yield per ton.	Gold from alluvial mines.	Total yield of gold.	Maximum yield per ton.	Average yield per man for 12 months, at $18 50 per oz.
					Tons.Cwt.Lbs	Oz.Dwt.Gr	Oz.Dwt.Gr	Oz.Dwt.Gr	Oz.Dwt.Gr	
Stormont, Isaac's Harbor.	94	3	2	1	1,122 2 0	1 15 15	....	1,999 0 2	8 10 18	$394 47
Wine Harbor	51	4	3	1	4,363 17 0	12 2	....	2,664 3 11	16 10 0	946 80
Sherbrooke	83	4	4	....	2,637 3 0	1 3 19	....	3,137 9 5	8 3 0	699 27
Tangier	50	5	2	3	681 10 0	18 7	117 9 0	741 7 15	9 6 21	274 00
Montagu.........	38	1	1	....	675 4 0	1 12 10	....	1,095 17 13	3 18 9	533 50
Waverley........	270	5	4	1	10,709 2 0	1 4 11	....	13,102 0 21	3 13 19	895 87
Oldham..........	65	5	4	1	2,409 15 0	10 7	....	1,242 6 21	10 15 3	353 52
Renfrew.........	35	5	3	2	1,114 10 0	14 17	....	820 12 23	7 17 12	436 60
Other and unproclaimed........	6	1	....	1	122 8 0	10 10	23 19 0	64 6 21	1 17 6	
	692	33	23	10	23,835 11 0	1 0 21	141 7 0	24,867 5 22	16 10 0	664 80

Abstract of gold mining statistics—1866.

Districts.	Average men employed.	Crushing mills employed Sept. 30, '66.	Steam power.	Water power.	Quartz, sand, and gravel crushed.	Yield per ton.	Gold from alluvial mines.	Total yield of gold.	Maximum yield per ton.	Average yield per man for 12 months, at $18,50 per oz.
					Tons.Cwt.Lbs	Oz.Dwt.Gr	Oz.Dwt.Gr	Oz.Dwt.Gr	Oz.Dwt.Gr	
Stormont, Isaac's Harbor.	34½	3	2	1	1,956 7 0	0 10 18	....	1,035 7 13	3 0 0	$565 91
Wine Harbor	35	4	3	1	2,192 8 0	11 4	....	1,224 13 1	87 0 0	647 27
Sherbrooke	69	4	4	....	2,684 1 0	1 22 0	....	5,157 14 17	16 6 16	1,382 86
Tangier..........	28	4	1	3	956 2 0	8 19	11 17 4	430 0 3	4 18 0	277 50
Montagu.........	26½	1	1	....	563 5 0	1 6 0	....	707 1 1	3 12 0	488 95
Waverley........	332	7	6	1	17;286 0 0	12 1	....	10,486 0 21	3 7 0	584 31
Oldham..........	36	7	5	2	964 2 0	16 2	....	776 12 4	6 3 19	399 6
Renfrew.........	94	7	5	2	4,181 7 0	19 23	....	4,176 3 17	9 18 0	821 90
Unproclaimed and other	12½	1	....	1	179 10 0	17 15	24 17 11	158 11 8	12 0 0	234 65
	667½	38	27	11	30,963 2 0	15 14	36 14 15	24,162 4 13	87 0 0	669 41

Abstract of gold mining statistics—1867.

Districts.	Average men employed.	Crushing mills in dist.	Steam power.	Water power.	Quartz, sand, and gravel crushed.	Yield per ton.	Gold from alluvial mines.	Total yield of gold.	Maximum yield per ton.	Average annual yield per man engaged in mining.
					Tons.Cwt.Lbs	Oz.Dwt.Gr	Oz.Dwt.Gr	Oz.Dwt.Gr	Oz.Dwt.Gr	
Isaac's Harbor ...	45	2	2	0	1,149 0 0	1 5 8	....	1,505 2 11	4 10 0	$618 73
Wine Harbor	33	4	3	1	1,667 0 0	8 13	....	764 9 9	26 13 8	428 60
Sherbrooke	99	5	5	0	5,800 0 0	1 9 8	....	8,522 8 11	11 13 5	1,592 58
Tangier..........	19	4	2	2	486 0 0	16 7	20 6 0	395 16 10	4 6 16	385 50
Montagu.........	19	1	1	0	214 0 0	1 19 0	....	417 13 21	2 9 20	406 60
Waverley........	181	5	4	1	11,299 0 0	7 7	....	4,134 18 17	1 12 18	492 63
Oldham..........	52	4	3	1	960 0 0	1 8 7	....	1,359 12 2	4 0 20	433 88
Renfrew.........	189	5	3	2	7,770 0 0	1 4 4	....	9,401 2 10	3 8 1	895 30
Uniacke	30	3	3	0	1,212 0 0	15 15	....	947 1 17	14 10 0	584 00
Unproclaimed and other districts..	9	2	1	1	117 0 0	1 3 4	26 15 15	135 0 21	2 0 0	278 55
Total......	676	35	27	8	30,673 0 0	17 23	49 1 15	27,583 6 9	26 13 8	765 00

As intimated elsewhere in this paper, operations in search of gold in Nova Scotia have been prosecuted almost invariably in the veins of quartz *in situ.* In the few localities where alluvial mining has been carried on the means employed have been, as in other countries, those of the cradle, long-tom, and sluice, but more especially the latter. But even in the few alluvial auriferous deposits which have yet been discovered free gold is only found in small quantity. In such places the surface soil is usually found to be profusely interspersed with fragments of auriferous quartz, with boulders and pebbles of what had been its enclosing rock. The processes referred to merely wash off the earthy matter from the mixed material, retaining the free gold and the fragments of quartz and other rocks. From the latter the quartz is separated and subjected to the stamping mill. This may seem a tedious process, and it requires much care; but in the few localities which have favored the operation, it has proved very remunerative. In some instances, and generally where the situation favored such a process, the whole of the surface material has been run through the stamping mill, as the more profitable mode of saving the gold contained in it.

The Nova Scotian gold, as taken from the matrix, is almost singularly free from alloy, a fact which, in a very material degree, exempts the gold hunter there from difficulties which beset him in many other parts of the world. As to the mode of reducing the auriferous quartz, slate, &c., and extracting the gold therefrom, numerous processes have been tried. For pulverizing quartz the first apparatus employed—not considering the rude and temporary appliances hurriedly improvised on the first discovery of gold—was the stamping mill. Since then, and more especially during the first two or three years of Nova Scotia's gold-mining history, numerous other contrivances, involving some variety of mechanical principles, have been tried. We have had improved specimens of the rude arrastra, the Chilian mill, the revolving pan and sphere, the "dry process" of pulverizing quartz by passing it through a rapidly revolving cylinder, and various combinations and varieties of these. Some processes which I have not had opportunities of inspecting have also been employed for a time. But all others have, as yet, been, by practical men, sooner or later discarded in favor of the old stamping mill.

In the appliances used for amalgamation there has been almost as great a variety, but a pretty nearly uniform process has eventually been adopted. Quicksilver is deposited in quantity in the stamper-boxes. As a thin stream of water runs continually into each stamper-box while the mill is in operation, the finer and lighter particles of the triturated gangue are being constantly washed out, through a wire gauze or finely perforated plate, upon a sloping table, the sides of which converge, and, at its lower end, conduct to a succession of sluice-boxes which form a gradual descent. The bottom and sides of this table and these sluice-boxes are covered with copper plates. In some mills, instead of sluice-boxes, there are provided shaking tables, the superior advantages of which yet remain, I think, to be proved. By this mode a greatly preponderating portion of the gold freed from its matrix never leaves the stamper-box, but amalgamates and remains there with the quicksilver. The particles of both metals, thrown out by the mechanical action of the machinery and the current of water, are caught upon the copper plates, over which, for a time, they are carried.

This is the mode of treatment which, thus far, has met with the most general approval. It is of not unfrequent occurrence that when a new comer from abroad enters a mining district he regards somewhat scornfully the simple processes I have briefly sketched; but it invariably happens that, after indulging in some—frequently very expensive—experiments in setting up "the latest improvements," he falls back into the old mode, or some very slight modification of it. That all the gold is saved by this treatment is more than any person would be justified in saying. For about the first year of gold mining in Nova Scotia most mills had in connection with them kilns for roasting the quartz before it was subjected to the stamps. It was discovered, however, or supposed to be, that no profit was made by this, and that, indeed, the balance, if any, was on the other side of the account.

It is certain that in most auriferous quartz veins mispickel (arsenical pyrites) is found, in some of them in large and numerous masses. It may be safely averred that all of this is impregnated with gold; and, owing to the difficulty, if not impossibility, of amalgamating any considerable portion of the gold so associated by the simple process above described, a considerable quantity must be lost. Latterly some proprietors of mines have carefully separated this arsenical pyrites from the tailings of their quartz mills, barrelled it up, and sent it to Europe, where it has been subjected to chemical treatment and has yielded, I have been led to believe, a good profit to the owner. I am not aware that a like treatment has yet come into use in Nova Scotia.

I must here observe that the sodium amalgam, of comparatively recent discovery, where experimented with in the mines of this province, has produced highly gratifying results, and is gradually creeping into general use.

OF MINES OTHER THAN GOLD.—In treating of the mineral resources of Nova Scotia other than auriferous deposits, and more especially of its coal fields, I find myself even more at a loss to speak definitely than in dealing with its gold mines. This difficulty is owing to the very imperfect character of the geological and mineralogical explorations that have yet taken place in the province. To explain this, again, I must be historical to the extent of a few sentences.

In 1826, at which time little or nothing was known of the geology and mineralogy of the •

country, all the minerals reserved to the crown in granted lands and all those in crown lands were granted by George IV to his brother, the late Duke of York, for a term of 60 years. This grant virtually transferred nearly all the mineral products of Nova Scotia. The property thus conveyed to the Duke of York eventually came into the hands of the "General Mining Association," a powerful English company. While the whole mineral resources of the country were thus locked up by a monopoly, little or no disposition was shown, either by the provincial government or private individuals, to ascertain what the extent of those resources was. At length, after years of irritation, probably on both sides, and some not very successful efforts on the part of the Nova Scotians to possess themselves of a share of the mineral wealth of their own country, an arrangement was effected between the provincial government and the General Mining Association in August, 1857, which was confirmed by the Nova Scotian legislature early in the ensuing year, and went immediately into effect. According to this arrangement the association were allowed to retain, with some ameliorations in the terms of their lease, all the coal seams contained in about 75 square miles, comprising the mines already opened and worked by them at Sydney, Point Aconi, Lingan, and Bridgport, in Cape Breton, the Albion mines in Pictou, and Springhill and The Joggins in Cumberland. The association, on their part, relinquished all claim whatsoever to the mines and minerals throughout the remainder of the province. Almost immediately upon the conclusion of this arrangement there commenced an activity previously unknown in Nova Scotia in exploring for minerals, and more especially for coal, outside of the tracts still · retained by the General Mining Association. Years must yet elapse before the results of this still actively continued exploration can enable us to form anything like a close approximation to an estimate of the area of Nova Scotia which is underlaid by available coal seams, or of the aggregate quantity of coal which may be extracted from those coal beds and put in the market. I shall, however, give a brief outline of what seem to be the possibilities of the country in this respect.

It has already been stated above that of the 18,600 square miles of the total area of the province of Nova Scotia about 10,000 square miles belong to the geological formation throughout which auriferous deposits are found. Let us deduct from the remaining surface of the province that portion which belongs to the new red sandstone formation, associated with trap rock. This is represented by a narrow strip of land varying from two to five miles in width, extending along the south shore of the Bay of Fundy, from Brier island to Cape Blouridon, and also some islands and isolated headlands on both sides of Minas basin and Cobequid bay. All the remainder of Nova Scotia belongs to the carboniferous formation. The productive coal measures of this formation naturally divide themselves into the following independent coal fields:

The *North Hants and South Colchester* coal basin presents no good, natural cross section, although it is bisected in nearly equal halves by the Shubenacadie river. Thin seams of coal have been discovered at several points near the margin of this basin, but no mines have ' been opened, and its value as a productive coal field yet remains to be proved.

The *North Colchester* field comprises a narrow strip between the Cobequid Hills, on the one side, and the shores of Minas basin and Cobequid bay on the other, and extending from the vicinity of Parrsborough to the confines of Pictou county. Coal has been mined to a small extent, but, although several seams have been discovered, they are so thin that to work them to any extent, in the present state of the coal and labor markets, would not prove remunerative.

The *Cumberland* coal field is much more extensive. At the western confines of this district, at a place called The Joggins, the shore of Chiegnecto bay affords a remarkably fine cross section of the whole formation. Here may be observed upwards of 70 coal seams, comprising an aggregate thickness of over 40 feet. The more important workable seams, taken in descending order, are of the respective thicknesses of five feet, one foot nine inches, two feet nine inches, five feet, four feet, and five feet, being six in all. Two of these seams are worked on the Joggins shore by the General Mining Association, who there hold four square miles of mining territory. From three to four miles east of the Joggins mine are the Victoria and Lawrence mines, on opposite sides of the navigable river Hebut. Further east, and fronting upon the navigable Macan river, is the Macan mine. On the east side of the same river and lying contiguous to each other are the mines of the Chiegnecto, the St. George, and the New York and Acadia companies. All of these mines have been opened within a comparatively recent period, and all are supposed to be worked upon some of the same seams which exhibit themselves upon the Joggins shore, although none of them conform in every particular to any of the beds found at the latter place.

Near Northumberland strait, the extreme eastern shore of Cumberland, some coal seams have been discovered which are supposed to be the equivalents of those seen at The Joggins, but none of workable thickness have there been exposed as yet.

At a place called Spring Hill, in the interior of this county, and near the northern base of the Cobequid Hills, about 20 miles southeast of The Joggins, the General Mining Association possess a tract of four square miles. A seam of excellent coal, 12 feet in thickness, has here been found, but no proper mine has yet been opened. The explorations made of late years by other lessees, outside of the association's tract, seem to indicate that there are several available coal seams in this vicinity; but the partial nature of those explorations and a very considerable degree of disturbance of the strata, which is a characteristic of the district and a serious difficulty to the explorer, precludes our forming anything but a vague estimate of either the number or extent of its coal beds.

The *Pictou* coal basin lies about the centre of the county of the same name. Considering how comparatively limited is its horizontal extent, it comprises an enormous aggregate thickness of coal beds. The most important seams of good coal known, as yet, in this district are of the respective thicknesses of 38, 22, 6, 11½, 1¼ ("oil coal,") 19, and 13 feet. In the centre of this district the General Mining Association have an area of four square miles, and at their colliery, known as the Albion mines, have carried on operations for many years. Surrounding this colliery on every side are others which have but recently been opened. Judging from its development thus far, the horizontal area underlaid by the above-mentioned seams, including what is believed to be an eastern extension of the Albion mines coal measures to Merigonish harbor, may be roughly estimated at not less than 30 square miles. Upon this space there are eight collieries now in operation, and preparations are being made for opening several others.   •

The *Antigonish* coal field comprises a small portion of the northeastern coast of the county of that name. Some small coal fields have been found in the vicinity of Pomquet harbor, and in consequence of this, explorations are being prospected with the sanguine hope of discovering one that can be worked with profit.

The productive measures of the *Inverness* coal field seem to be confined, for the most part, to a narrow band of country near the coast. A mine has recently been opened at Port Hood upon a seam of good coal, averaging six feet in thickness. Other coal seams, varying from three to seven feet in thickness, are found along the coast at Mabon, Broad Cove, and Chimney Corner. Although showing no extensive deposit on the shore, these beds, like the one being worked at Port Hood, dip seaward and are probably the outcrops of an extensive coal field under the waters of the Gulf of St. Lawrence. In the southern part of this county, along the river Inhabitants, coal has been found in several places, and there are promising indications of a valuable deposit of that mineral, but, owing to the comparative remoteness of the place from navigable water and the existence of so much coal elsewhere in the province in more favored situations, little exploration has been made in this locality.

This River Inhabitants district may more poperly be considered a northern extension of the Richmond coal field, which comprises, along with the tract just mentioned, all the western and middle portion of Richmond county. Here; all along the north side of Lennox Passage, from St. Peters west to the Strait of Canso, good indications of coal are found, although the stratification is, in places, very much disturbed. At Seacoal bay, in the south western part of the county, a mine has been opened upon a bed of coal and bituminous shale, nearly 12 feet in thickness, and of which four feet only are worked as a coal seam. The dip is here nearly vertical.

The Richmond mine is four miles inland, and northward of the last mentioned. Here two seams of three and four feet respectively are being worked. Their dip, as at Seacoal bay, is nearly vertical.

Victoria county has also its special coal field, isolated from any that have yet been, or will hereafter be described. Coal has been discovered on the north side of St. Patrick's channel, in the vicinity of the Wagamatkook and Baddeck rivers; but no mine has yet been opened, nor have explorations been there prosecuted to any extent.

The last, and in all probability most extensive and most important coal field which I shall have to describe, is that of Cape Breton. It extends along the eastern coast from Cape Dauphin, near the southeastern extremity of Victoria county to an unknown point under the waters of Mira bay, off South Head or Mira Gage, a distance of about 40 miles. Along this whole coast band, the productive coal measures are found extending inland for a distance of from seven to nine miles. The contained coal beds dip northeastward, thus indicating the more than probable existence of an immense body of coal beneath the sea. Notwithstanding the explorations which have been prosecuted with spirit and diligence for some years past, it is impossible as yet to state with confidence the number of coal seams of sufficient dimensions to be profitably worked in this fine district. I may state that not less than 20 of these seams have been opened and worked, and that these opened seams comprise an aggregate thickness of over 100 feet of superior coal. The whole district of these productive measures covers a horizontal area of from 250 to 300 square miles. All that portion of the district immediately adjoining the coast is under lease, 'and there are 16 collieries here in operation. These are all of recent origin, except those of the General Mining Association at North Sidney, Lingan, and Bridgport. Here is the largest tract retained by this association. It covers all the land extending along the line of coast from the north side of Boularderie island to a point about a mile south of Bridgport basin, and comprises over 60 quare miles. A cross section of the association's ground, on the north side of Sidney harbor above, shows no less than 34 seams of coal; but of these only four have yet been worked. I may observe that all the coal yet found in Nova Scotia is soft bituminous coal.

In our present still very limited knowledge of the real extent of the productive coal measures in Nova Scotia and their available contents in coal, any estimates of either the one or the other might be so remote an approximation to the truth as to be of very little practical value. It can only be said, in general terms, that the circumstances of that Province point to an enormous future development of that branch of mining.

The following figures showing the total amount of coal raised and shipped, in Nova Scotia, in tons and hundred weights from 1827 to 1867, inclusive, will exhibit the progress of its trade in this particular:

Years.	Tons.	Cwt.	Years.	Tons.	Cwt.
1827	11,491	......	1848	170,518	1
1828	19,429	17	1849	158,955	10
1829	20,252	12	1850	163,723	8
1830	23,240	6	1851	139,976	13
1831	34,424	8	1852	171,821	18
1832	46,585	6	1853	196,935	17
1833	59,497	4	1854	213,250	16
1834	46,677	12	1855	216,338	3
1835	51,813	5	1856	231,934	7
1836	98,427	3	1857	267,808	17
1837	109,347	12	1858	289,618	..
1838	97,938	14	1859	267,496	..
1839	133,928	11	1860	304,129	..
1840	98,267	17	1861	334,543	15
1841	136,110	9	1862	393,631	5
1842	119,478	12	1863	424,425	2
1843	97,200	12	1864 (9 months)	406,699	..
1844	99,993	14	1865	651,256	14
1845	137,908	13	1866	601,302	2
1846	134,393	12	1867	542,127	..
1847	183,099	13			

The slight falling off during the last two years is to be attributed to the abrogation of the "reciprocity treaty" between the Provinces and the United States.

The law of Nova Scotia relative to coal mines, as well as to all other mines other than gold, may be briefly summed up thus: The first step to be taken by the party intending to invest is to apply to the department of mines for a "license to search" upon whatever ground he may have selected for that purpose. The application must be accompanied by a payment of $20, and the filing of a bond to make good any damage done to private lands, and the license is not to cover more than five square miles, and it holds good for one year. At the expiration of this license, the holder thereof may, out of the ground covered by it, select one square mile; this area to be enlarged under certain special circumstances, over which, upon the payment of $50, he can obtain a "license to work," which holds good for two years. If, during this period, he shall have commenced "effective mining operations," he is entitled to receive a lease, terminable in 1886, but renewable. On such leases there is reserved a royalty of 10 cents on every ton of 2,240 pounds of coal; eight cents on every ton of iron, and five per cent. on all other minerals except gold, the royalty upon which has already been stated.

I may here add a few remarks as to the presence in Nova Scotia of the other more important reserved minerals. Copper has been found at several localities. Mining operations have been carried on for some years past in a bed of cupriferous clay, containing nodules of copper, in the carboniferous formations, at Tatamagouche, Colchester county. As this happens to be a place where the minerals have been granted with the soil, I have no reliable means of knowing what degree of success has attended the venture. What were considered promising indications were found a few years since, at Cheticamp, Inverness, and a Copper Mining Company commenced work there; but their operations have not yet proved successful. This mineral is also found in thin veins and detached masses, in the form of native copper and of the gray sulphuret, green carbonate, and oxide of that metal, at numerous points in the trap rock, on the shores of the bay of Fundy. At some localities in the vicinity of Polson's lake and the head waters of Salmon river, ou the confines of Antigonish and Guysborough counties, there are to be found large and numerous masses of copper ore, yielding from 5 to 20 per cent. of metal; but no real lode has yet been discovered.

At Gay's river, near the northern bounds of Halifax county, the boulders of lower carboniferous rock scattered through the surface soil over a tract of country considerable as to extent, as well as the soil itself, are profusely interspersed with galena, seeming to indicate the vicinity of an important lode of that mineral. Washed samples of this ore afforded 17$\frac{1}{2}$ per cent. of lead, and this lead gave 11$\frac{1}{2}$ ounces per ton of silver.

The only other useful mineral known to exist in quantity in Nova Scotia, of which mention need be made, is iron. On this head I will make some extracts from a work by the writer of this paper, entitled "Nova Scotia considered as a field for emigration," published in 1858:

The most western deposit of any extent yet discovered occurs at Clements, on the south side of Annapolis basin. The outcrop of the vein may be traced on the surface for the distance of a mile, with an average thickness of nine feet six inches. The ore consists of scales of specular iron, firmly cemented together and mixed with silicious and calcareous matter, and it has been in part converted by heat into magnetic iron ore. It yields from 33 to 40 per cent. of cast iron, the quality of which is said to be very superior. * * * * * * A bed of iron ore occurs at Nictau, also in the county of Annapolis, and is similar to that found at Clements. There are several parallel veins at this place, varying from 4 to 10 feet in thickness. Six of these have been examined and accurately defined, and the ore contains 55.3 per cent. of iron of excellent quality.

*   *   *   *   *   *   *

The next great deposit of iron ore which we will mention is found on the southern slope of the Cobequid hills. This deposit, considering its extent and the variety and quality of its ores, may be pronounced the most important in the Province. That part of it to which attention has been more particularly directed lies between the Debert river and a point some two miles westward of the Great Village river, a distance, in all, of about 10 miles. Between these points the vein extends nearly east and west, and at a distance of from five to eight miles from the shore of Cobequid bay. It consists of a veinstone of the species of ore called *ankerite*, associated with *spathose iron*, surrounding and including a number of other varieties of ore.

*   * The whole vein is of very irregular width. At one spot on the bank of the Great Village river it is 120 feet wide, whilst at another, not far from the most eastern point to which the vein has been traced, it attains a breadth of over 500 feet. Its breadth is unequal at various intermediate points where measurements have been made. The length of this vein is not yet ascertained; its continuation may be seen near Five islands, 20 miles westward of Great Village river, so that the vein is *known* to extend a distance of about 30 miles in length. It is not at all improbable that upon continued examination it will be found to extend along the whole length of the Cobequid range of hills. *   *   * The iron made from these ores is found to be equal to any in the world in the rare properties requisite for making good steel. *   *   *

A very extensive deposit of iron ore, of a description similar to that of Nictau, is found at East river, Pictou, and within 10 miles distance of the Albion coal mines on that river. The vein at this place is 16 feet in thickness. The situation of this deposit, like that of the Cobequid hills, affords every facility for the profitable manufacture of iron.

Iron ore, in the forms of red ochre, red hematite, and brown hematite, is found on the Shubenacadie near its mouth. It has also been found in small quantities in several other places, affording good reason to believe that further extensive deposits of that valuable mineral will be discovered upon a more general research into the mineral wealth of Nova Scotia.

Recent explorations have fully verified this prediction ; yet Londonderry, on the southern flank of the Cobequids, is the only place in the province where an iron mine is worked. At this place, known as the "Acadian mines," blast furnaces were erected about 17 years since, and the manufacture of charcoal iron has continued ever since.

I will only add in conclusion that by far the largest proportion of the surface of Nova Scotia, taken as a whole, is yet an unexplored territory, and that this remark applies especially to the large area of metamorphic rock, in the explored portions of which gold and iron are found in such abundance and under such favoring circumstances. From what has already been discovered it is only reasonable to believe that the country abounds to an almost singular degree in mineral wealth.

I have the honor to be your obedient servant,

PIERCE S. HAMILTON.

J. W. TAYLOR, Esq., *Washington.* ·

SECTION V.

Comparative statement of rates of duty on imports between the United States and Victoria, Australia.

Articles.	Rates of duty.	
	United States.	Victoria.
Beer, ale, porter, &c., in bottles.....	35 cents per gallon..............	12 cts per gallon.
casks......	20 cents per gallon..............	Do.
Butter ....,.......	4 cents per pound..............	2 cts per pound.
Bacon ....·........	2 cents per pound..............	Do.
Cigars.............................	$3 per pound	$1 20 per pound.
Coffee ....·......................	5 cents per pound..............	4 cts per pound.
Cocoa	8 cents per pound..............	Do.
Chocolate	6 cents per pound..............	Do.
Candles, adamantine	5 cents per pound..............	2 cts per pound.
wax......................	8 cents per pound..............	Do.
all other kinds	2¼ cents per pound.............	Do.
Cheese............................	4 cents per pound..............	Do.
Confectionery, value above 30 cents per pound.	50 per cent.	Do.
Doors.............................	35 per cent.	24 cents each.
Fruits, dried......................	10 per cent.	2 cts per pound.
preserved	30 per cent.	Do.
Hams	2 cents per pound..............	Do.
Lard	2 cents per pound.............	Do.
Maccaroni and vermicelli	30 per cent.	Do.

Comparative statement of rates of duty on imports, &c.—Continued.

Articles.	Rates of duty.	
	United States.	Victoria.
Nuts...............................	2 cents per pound............:.....	Not including co-coa, 2 cts per lb.
Meats and fish, prepared............	30 per cent......................	2 cts per pound.
Soap, toilet and shaving............	10 cents per lb. and 25 per cent ..	Do.
not otherwise provided for.....	1 cent per pound and 30 per cent .	Do.
Starch......	3 cents per pound and 20 per cent.	Do.
Sweetmeats	40 per cent......................	Do.
Wheat..............................	20 cents per bushel..............	18 cts per cwt.
Rye and barley....................	15 cents per bushel..............	Do.
Indian corn, maize, and oats	10 cents per bushel......,......	Do.
Hops	5 cents per pound	4 cts per pound.
Malt...`...........................	20 per cent......................	12 cts per bushel.
Oil, illuminating...................	40 cents per gallon.............	6 cts per gallon.
petroleum or rock...............	20 cents per gallon.............	Do.
crude coal....................	15 cents per gallon.............	Do.
linseed, flaxseed, hempseed, and rapeseed.	23 cents per gallon.............	Do.
neatsfoot, whale, &c......	20 per cent......................	Do.
croton	$1 per pound	Do.
olive, salad, and castor..........	$1 per gallon	Do.
cloves	$2 per pound....................	Do.
cognac..........................	$4 per ounce	Do.
anise	50 cents per pound.............	Do.
almonds ......-..............	$1 50 per pound	Do.
amber, crude	10 cents per pound.............	Do.
rectified.................	20 cents per pound.............	Do.
bay leaves	$17 50 per pound.	Do.
bergamot and cassia...........	$1 per pound.	Do.
caraway, citronella, fennel, lemon, and orange.	50 cents per pound.............	Do.
fruit......	$2 per pound	Do.
cinnamon	$2 50 per pound ....:....	Do.
cubebs.........................	$1 per pound`............	Do.
juniper.........................	25 cents per pound.............	Do
thyme	30 cents per pound.............	Do.
roses	$1 50 per ounce	Do.
valerian	$1 50 per pound	Do.
not otherwise provided for	50 per cent	Do.
Opium............................	$2 50 per pound	$2 40 per pound.
for smoking	100 per cent....................	Do.
Rice..............................	2¼ cents per pound.............	48 cts per cwt.
Salt	18 and 24 cents per cwt..........	$4 80 per ton.
beef and pork..................	1 cent per pound...............	$1 20 per cwt.
mackerel.....................	$2 per barrel	Do.
salmon	$3 per barrel	Do.
fish, all other kinds in barrels ...	$1 per barrel	Do.
Snuff	50 cents per pound.............	48 cts per pound.
Spirits and wines	20 cents to $2 50 per gallon......	$2 40 per gallon.
Wines in bottles.	$3 to $6 per dozen	72 cts per gallon.
Cologne and other perfumery........	$3 per gallon and 50 per cent.....	Do.
Sugar	3 to 5 cents per pound..........	72 cts per cwt.
Molasses, sirup of sugar cane........	2¼ cents per pound.............	Do.
Tea	25 cents per pound.............	6 cts per pound.
Tobacco, manufactured.............	50 cents per pound.............	48 cts per pound.
unmanufactured	35 cents per pound............:	24 cts per pound.
Vegetables	10 per cent.....................	2 cts per pound.
Varnish...........................	50 cts pr gal. and 20 and 25 pr cent.	48 cts per gallon.
Vinegar	10 cents per gallon.............	12 cts per gallon.
Wood, manufactured...............	20 per cent.....................	Window sashes, 24 cts per pair.

Comparative statement of rates of duty on imports, &c.—Continued.

Articles.	Rates of duty.	
	United States.	Victoria.
Articles of gold	40 per cent.	$1 92 pr oz. troy.
silver and platina	40 per cent	24 cts pr oz. troy.
Apparel and slops made up wholly or in part of silk.	50 and 60 per cent	10 per cent.
Apparel, &c., made up wholly or in part of ·wool.	24 cents per lb. and 40 per cent ..	Do.
Apparel &c., made up wholly or in part of linen.	35 and 40 per cent	Do.*
Boots and shoes	30 per cent	Do.
Brushes	40 per cent	Do.
Building materials, boards, planks, staves, scantlings, hewn and sawed timber, &c.	20 per cent	Do.
Carpeting, value $1 25 and under	70 cents per square yard	Do.
over $1 25	80 cents per square yard	Do.
various kinds	35 to 50 per cent	Do.
Oilcloths	30 to 40 per cent	Do.
Carriages	35 per cent	Do.
Copperware, brassware, and tinware	35 and 40 per cent	Do.
Cordage	2¼ and 3 cents per pound	Do.
China and porcelain	50 per cent	Do.
Earthenware	25 per cent	Do.
Furniture, household	35 per cent	Do.
Furs	10 to 20 per cent	Do.
Glass	¾ to 60 cents per square foot	Do.
Glassware	35 to 40 per cent	Do.
Gloves	50 per cent	Do.
Glue	20 per cent	Do.
Hats, caps, and bonnets	35 to 60 per cent	Do.
Hosiery	20 cents per lb. and 30 per cent	Do.
Jewelry	25 per cent	Do.
Lead, sheet, pipe, &c	2¾ cents per pound	Do.
Leatherware	35 to 50 per cent	Do.
Marble, manufactures of	50 per cent	Do.
white statuary, &c.	$1 per cubic foot and 20 per cent	Do.
Matches	35 per cent	Do.
Metal, manufactures of	35 per cent	Do
Millinery, not otherwise provided for.	35 per cent	Do.
Musical instruments	30 per cent	Do.
Tapioca and spices	20 per cent	Do.
Sago	1¼ cents per pound	Do
Arrowroot	30 per cent	Do.
Pepper	18 cents per pound	Do.
Ginger	50 per cent	Do.
Plated metal	35 per cent	Do.
Saddles and harness	35 per cent	Do.
Tarpaulins	20 per cent	Do.
Japanned ware	40 per cent	Do.
Wooden and other toys	50 per cent	Do.
Watches	25 per cent	Do.
Clocks	35 per cent	Do.
Willow and wooden ware	35 per cent	Do.
Woollen blankets	24 cents per lb. and 40 per cent	Do.
Woollen bags	24 cents per lb. and 40 per cent	5 per cent.
Anchors	2¼ cents per pound	Exempt.
Animals and birds	Exempt	Do.
Books	25 per cent	Do.
Bristles	15 cents per pound	Do.
hair	1 cent per pound	Do.
Baggage, personal	Exempt	Do.

Comparative statement of rates of duty on imports, &c.—Continued.

Articles.	Rates of duty.	
	United States.	Victoria.
Chain cables	2½ cents per pound	Exempt.
Coal, bituminous	$1 25 per ton	Do.
all other kinds	40 cents per ton	Do.
Coke	25 per cent	Do.
Coins and bullion	Exempt	Do.
Copper ore	25 per cent	Do.
when imported for U. S. mint	Exempt	Do.
Cotton, in the piece	35 per cent	Do.
raw	3 cents per pound	Do.
Fish, fresh	50 cents per cwt	Do.
Flax	$15 per ton	Do.
Guano and other manures	Exempt	Do.
Hatter's plush	25 per cent	Do.
Hemp	$10 to $40 per cwt	Do.
Hides and skins	10 per cent	Do.
Iron, scrap	$8 per ton	Do.
pig	$9 per ton	Do.
bar	1 and 1½ cents per pound	Do.
rod	1¼ and 1½ cents per pound	Do.
hoop	1¼ and 1¾ cents per pound	Do.
sheet	1¼ to 3 cents per pound	Do.
railroad bars	70 cents per cwt	Do.
Jute	$10 per ton	Do.
Kerosene shale	40 cents per gallon	Do.
Lead, ore	1½ cents per pound	Do.
bars	2 cents per pound	Do.
scrap	1½ cents per pound	Do.
Linen	35 to 40 per cent	Do.
Oil, palm and cocoa	10 per cent	Do.
Paper, printing	20 per cent	Do.
wrapping	30 per cent	Do.
Pitch	20 per cent	Do.
Plants, medicinal	20 per cent	Do.
ornamental	30 per cent	Do.
for dying	Exempt	Do.
Printer's ink	35 per cent	Do.
Quicksilver	15 per cent	Do.
Rags	Exempt	Do.
Resin	20 per cent	Do.
Saltpetre	3 cents per pound	Do.
Soda, ash	½ cent per pound	Do.
caustic	1 cent per pound	Do.
Specimens natural history, &c	Exempt	Do.
Steel	2¼ to 3¼ cts pr lb. and 10 pr cent	Do.
Stones, building	20 per cent	Do.
Sulphur, flour of	$20 per ton and 15 per cent	Do.
Tallow	1 cent per pound	Do.
Tar	20 per cent	Do.
Timber, logs	20 per cent	Do.
Tin	15 per cent	Do.
Wire, steel	2¼ and 3 cts pr lb. and 20 pr cent	Do.
Wool	3 to 10 cts per lb. and 10 per cent.	Do.
Woollen cloths	24 cents per lb. and 40 per cent	Do.
Yellow metal sheeting and zinc	3 cents per pound	Do.

INDEX: